In Every Corner Sing

In Every Corner Sing

A Poet's Corner Collection

Malcolm Guite

CANTERBURY
PRESS

Norwich

First published in 2018 by the Canterbury Press Norwich
Editorial office
3rd Floor, Invicta House,
108–114 Golden Lane,
London EC1Y 0TG.

Canterbury Press is an imprint of Hymns Ancient & Modern Ltd
(a registered charity)
13A Hellesdon Park Road, Norwich,
Norfolk, NR6 5DR, UK
www.canterburypress.co.uk

British Library Cataloguing in Publication data
A catalogue record for this book is available
from the British Library

978 1-78622-097-4

Printed and bound in Great Britain by
CPI Group (UK) Ltd

Contents

Preface

Preface

It has been a pleasure to gather together these fugitive pieces, little glimpses and reflections from all corners of the country, curious corners of my mind, and a few of the odd corners and alleyways of our rich literature, the corners where the poets repose, sometimes confer, but always and everywhere sing.

I was both honoured and daunted when the *Church Times* asked me to follow on from Ronald Blythe's wonderful back-page column 'Word from Wormingford'. Nobody can follow Ronnie Blythe, but I was willing to try at least to fill the space, and I knew I shared with him some feeling for the beauty of the world around us and some common companionship with the poets whose music undergirds all our songs, especially George Herbert and Thomas Traherne, so my weekly column, gathered together here, was christened 'Poet's Corner'.

Reading through these pieces again is like being given back a little of my own life, seized back from seizing time, letting me repose again on a bench in Aldeburgh, a book room in Hawarden, a bridge in my lovely village of Linton.

Though each piece was written in and for its own moment, I see that certain themes and motifs have emerged and played with one another across the weeks of the year. One is the gift and grace of running water, so beautifully pictured in Roger Wagner's lovely painting, 'The River of God', on the cover of this book. For flowing water always gives me some sense of the hidden wellspring from which we all arise, the fresh renewing fount of all things, just upstream of utterance, a sense that though time never ceases to flow from and through us, we are as close now, as we will ever be, to its eternal source. And that motif itself speaks of another, emerging clearly as I read these pieces through: the sense that everything we see 'out there' is also somehow hidden deep within us – the trees, the hills, the dewdrops on a blade of grass – are emblems of our inner life that could not be expressed or known without them: everything 'out there' is also 'in here'. A third theme to emerge is a sense of companionship with other poets and writers, present and past. And in that sense it really has been 'Poets' Corner'. In that corner of Westminster Abbey we can see the monuments to all the great poets and writers whom we know and love, but it is not the outward and visible, the letters carved in stone, that count, it is the inward and spiritual: the poems written, and then sung in the heart. Time and again as I was writing these pieces, I sensed George Herbert in one corner, and Seamus Heaney in another, giving me the words I needed just when I needed them. William Hazlitt was there when I reflected on the pleasure my books give me on a winter's night, and Thomas Traherne met me with wisdom on London Bridge on the night that such terrible violence was inflicted there.

I hope that all these themes and motifs – the play of and grace of water, the gift of an emblem, the companionship of the poets – will be as richly and happily available to readers of this volume as they were to me when I wrote these little corner-pieces, and that something in each of them will stir and sing.

1

Eternity in Huntingdon

I once glimpsed eternity in Huntingdon.

I can be more specific. I was picking up litter around the church I used to serve on the Oxmoor Estate. Perhaps because its grounds formed a short-cut between the pub and the chippy, or maybe because it had eaves and a porch under which you could shelter from the rain, a lot of stuff used to get discarded there. Not just the fish-and-chip papers and other dropped or regurgitated takeaways, but sometimes, more sadly, the used needles that were testimony to so much waste and exploitation.

As I was gingerly picking up a piece of newspaper on top of which various unpleasant things had been deposited, I became curious about a word in large print, part of which I could glimpse beneath the detritus. I shifted things slightly so as to be able to read it, and what I read, unexpectedly, and in capital letters, was 'ETERNITY'.

I took it as a sign of sorts, a gesture in the direction of hope. I remembered that phrase in Ecclesiastes about how everything flourishes and fails in its time, but God has set eternity in our hearts.

I thought about the good people on that estate, sold and selling cheap, undervalued, dismissed to a margin, on an estate labelled 'overspill' as though they were no more than the stuff spilled over that newspaper.

I thought about what it might be that was cluttering up and

covering over the eternity that God had set in their hearts, about what it might take to reveal it.

I thought about how the drugs themselves – the brief highs, the getting out of it, the repeated self-medication – were all in their own way trying to find, but only covering more thoroughly, that deep-buried eternity.

I even began to wonder if I might be called to see through the clutter and read that inner word out for them, or help them find and read it for themselves.

All this might have turned into a glowing little sermon illustration right then and there, had not some more of the detritus fallen away from the paper and revealed the rest of the message: 'ETERNITY by Calvin Klein'.

There's not much you can do when you are recovering from bathos like that, but I finished the job, put away my dustpan and broom, and glanced wryly up at the cross on the church roof.

And it was after that, when the congregation came – almost all of us, in one way or another, the walking wounded – and the bread was broken and shared, it was then that together, without the help of advertising or the wearing of any scents, just ourselves and Someone else in that dilapidated place, we glimpsed eternity, just enough of it to make the walk back in to time more bearable.

2

Upstream

The village of Linton, where I live, is blessed with five bridges. I can cross over one of them on an early stroll through the place, delighting in the clarity of the stream below, the light glancing off its ripples and dimples, as it runs over shallows, purling and turning in the wake of a scurrying duckling, and think, 'I'm glad I saw that,' only to find that, five minutes later, the river is back, rippling ahead of me and saying 'Look, look! Here's another bridge: cross me again!'

Even when I walk beside it for a while, it's always diving in and out of cover and emerging to surprise me, like a very young child playing peek-a-boo.

These are the upper reaches of the Granta, and it's hard to imagine that this playful little stream, curling and chattering round the church and the green, is the same one that will later run a little straighter, a little deeper, but still young and lovely, along the famous stretch of Grantchester meadows, and thence to Cambridge, where it will be very grown up, change its name to the Cam, and flow in stately and straightened procession between the arches and chapels of the old colleges. There it becomes the river that Milton saw when he was a student, and solemnly hailed as

Camus, reverend sire ... footing slow,
His mantle hairy, and his bonnet sedge ...

I also make the daily journey downstream from Linton to Cambridge, and, although I don't change my name, I do, I suppose, change my garb and my demeanour. Perhaps I, too, become a little straightened.

But there I have the pleasure of meeting, listening to, and occasionally teaching, the young. They arrive in Cambridge from many places, and, while they are all always themselves, they also acquire something of the character of the place through which they flow collectively. They, too, are straightened a little, in good ways and bad.

Contrary to the popular image, these students work very hard, and their energies are gathered and channelled, especially in the summer term when so much might invite them to a little playful meandering. Instead, I see them, concentrating and deepening, between the high banks of bookshelves in the library.

But sometimes, when they drop into my room to see their chaplain, they tell me stories of where they've been and where they've come from. They reach back into childhood and give me a glimpse of the playfulness, the energy, and the mischief that lie upstream of their Cambridge days.

On other days, they come to me clouded or troubled, when their lives seem muddied and unclear, and I wish, a little subversively perhaps, that we could both be taken upstream for a moment and enjoy again that early combination of clarity and playfulness. Just occasionally, before I turn upstream again to Linton, there's a moment in prayer or silence when we both find ourselves much further upstream, up at the fresh and playful source from which everything flows.

3

A Mystery Cat

I had an interesting encounter one evening with our college cat. A strong, self-possessed stray, Buster, like one or two students I have known, sauntered into college one day as if he already owned the place, and simply allowed us to adopt him.

He is, of course, a fixture now, and so won the heart of the previous Mistress that she had his portrait painted when she left, and gave it to the college as a leaving present. Now his image adorns the corridors alongside the great and the good – doubtless, from his point of view, raising the tone.

He is usually curled up comfortably near the Porters' Lodge or in some corridor, condescending to be admired by a new circle of students; but on this particular evening he attended chapel. Our preacher at evensong was in the midst of a very eloquent sermon whose nub and pith was that no human eloquence was adequate to the mystery of God.

Indeed, mystery was his theme: we begin and end in mystery, we are a mystery even to ourselves, and, if no words or music can ever sum up or define the mystery of even one person, then how much less the mystery of God.

He was just adducing the undoubted authority of Aquinas on this point when I became aware, amid the gravity of the subject, of a strange levity in the choir. Smiles and a little wave of suppressed giggles passed along the front row.

And then I caught sight of Buster, who had made his way up

into the sanctuary and was now elegantly disporting himself, just behind the preacher.

I remembered that only the previous term I had read from that pulpit verses from Christopher Smart's beautiful *Jubilate Agno*:

For I will consider my Cat Jeoffry.

For he is the servant of the Living God, duly and daily serving him.

For at the first glance of the glory of God in the East he worships in his way.

Perhaps rumours of that reading had reached Buster.

The preacher, too, became aware that something was afoot, and at that moment Buster came round into his field of vision. He paused in his preaching, and then he did a beautiful thing. He smiled, and, with his own elegant gesture and light touch, he acknowledged the mystery cat.

Thereafter, the sermon, no less learned, had a lightness to its depth, and perhaps we better apprehended its conclusion: that life itself, and all things worth having, are given, not striven for, are never fully predicted or understood, but appear unexpectedly as graces to be apprehended, mysteries to be acknowledged.

Buster seemed satisfied that he had achieved what he came for; for he wandered down to my stall, and, seeing beside me a vacant chair, upholstered in a beautiful red velvet that very fetchingly set off his own more restrained collegiate black and white, he hopped neatly up and made himself comfortable. It had but recently been vacated and was, indeed, still warm; for it was, as surely Buster knew, the visiting preacher's stall.

4

Tuning Up

Restringing a guitar is an absorbing and, at the same time, relaxing thing to do. My guitar, like its owner, has had its adventures, dents, and scrapes, and carries, to put it politely, the patina of age. But, thanks to the occasional new set of strings, it still sounds and resounds as it should – perhaps better than it did to begin with.

What makes restringing seem so strangely restorative?

Perhaps the outward actions: the slackening of the old strings, the stretching of the new, and the gradual tautening until there is a resonance – pitched as before, but brightened now, and clarified. Perhaps there is some inner correspondence: the restringer is himself restrung, the tuner tuned.

That sequence – slackening, changing, renewing, and retuning – gives a better account of what happens on a good holiday, a good retreat, or even a good night's sleep, than the usual flat cliché about 'recharging my battery'. I'd rather be picked up and played than just left plugged in somewhere.

Touching the harmonics to tune my old Gibson sometimes seems to summon other resonances, too. As I tauten the strings, I think of George Herbert's lovely lines:

> Awake, my lute, and struggle for thy part
> With all thy art.
> The cross taught all wood to resound his name,
> Who bore the same.

> His stretched sinews taught all strings, what key
> Is best to celebrate this most high day.

The strings of Herbert's lute were literally visceral: organic lines of gut, which, stretched and struck, set up a sympathetic resonance in the wood. I love Herbert's theology of resonance; of our tuned response to the striking music of Christ's sacrifice. His language is itself so resonant: 'The cross taught all wood to resound his name' carries in the word 'taught' the other sense of the tautness of the strings. Even on Easter Day, Herbert looks back to Good Friday, and in that light sees Christ's 'stretched sinews' on the cross making a new music.

I am sure that Herbert was a better musician than I, but I take comfort that he on his lute, as I on my old guitar, had to 'struggle for his part'.

When I hear the rich music that rings out from Herbert's life, music caught so well in John Drury's book *Music at Midnight*, I sometimes feel that all I can manage with my own life, as with my old guitar, is a little tentative tuning up.

Then the echo of another poet-priest comes to my aid. I remember John Donne's gentle suggestion that all we do here, and the best of all we hear, is itself no more than tuning up for heaven:

> Since I am coming to that holy room,
> Where, with thy choir of saints for evermore,
> I shall be made thy music; as I come
> I tune the Instrument here at the door …

5

Mistaken Identity

Something strange, but strangely beautiful, happened to me the other day when I was hearing mass in Clare Priory. I say 'hearing' because, as an Anglican guest in that lovely old Roman Catholic house, which has made me so welcome, I knew I could not receive the sacrament, but I still delighted to be in its presence. I like making retreats there, amid those ruins come to life again, because I so often feel myself to be just that – a ruin come to life again.

What happened was this. When we stood to share the Peace, a very well-dressed man, whom I had noticed glancing at me at various points in the service with a look of kind concern, slipped a folded paper discreetly into my hand as he shook it. I couldn't look then and there; so I slipped it quietly into my pocket, and returned to my place as the service continued.

After the mass was ended, and we went in peace, I took the paper from my pocket – it turned out to be a tenner! I was nonplussed at first, and then it suddenly dawned on me that he had taken me, or mistaken me, for a tramp, for one of those gentlemen of the road whom the religious houses of England still occasionally shelter and set on their way again.

Well, I suppose my appearance was against me. I may have been, I confess, a little dishevelled (shevelling was never my strong point), and perhaps my longish white hair and beard and my favourite old tweed greatcoat all contributed to the mistaken identity. I suddenly recalled the day, some 40 years ago, when I set off from school for my university interview, wearing a new-bought suit and having actually combed my hair, and, as I left, one of the schoolmasters opened a window and shouted after me 'Guite, you look like a tramp who is pretending not to be!' (they didn't go in for 'affirmation' in those days), and I realized why even my wife has given up on keeping me tidy as a lost cause.

But what to do? My benefactor had long since gone, and, even if I found him, it would only have embarrassed him to return the money. Well, I thought, perhaps I can be a courier, and I can make a special delivery to the next 'gentleman of the road' I meet, the one for whom this gift was really intended.

It didn't take long. I don't remember beggars in Cambridge when I was a student in the 1970s, but now I counted seven in my short walk from the bus station to another bus stop. I made the first one's day with my recorded delivery, but something strange was happening: as I met the other six, I somehow found there was a little more money in my pocket than I thought, that my wallet was somehow a little easier to open – or was it my eyes that had been opened, too?

6

Rage and Beauty

My Saturday began amid the lush green hills of Hereford-shire, where, as Chesterton says:

> The soft feet of the blessed go
> In the soft western vales,
> The road the silent saints accord,
> The road from Heaven to Hereford,
> Where the apple wood of Hereford
> Goes all the way to Wales.

I had been invited to speak at the Traherne festival, and start-ed my day gazing from the church porch at Credenhill across to the Hay Bluff, utterly open to all that Thomas Traherne had seen when he stood there and glimpsed 'the orient and immortal wheat ... and young men glittering and sparkling Angels, and maids strange seraphic pieces of life and beauty' – the eternal, for that immortal poet, always and everywhere translucent through time.

But my day did not end there. It ended in Southwark. For that evening I travelled from Hereford to Paddington and thence to London Bridge, and walked through the Borough Market, minutes before the terrorist attacks.

I made my way to the Dean's house in readiness for a Pentecost sermon. It was never preached. I had just been welcomed into that lovely house by the Globe Theatre when suddenly the phones buzzed, the texts came through, the

21

sirens sounded outside as police boats sped up the river, and the emergency was upon us.

As soon as he grasped what was happening, the Dean left the house and walked back towards danger to see if he could open the cathedral. But he was held back by the police and returned, bringing a distressed Muslim friend with him, and all we could do was pray.

As the first shaky footage from mobile phones came through on the news, I found myself as utterly open to the shock and horror of those woundings I had missed by minutes as I had been to the lucent beauty of Credenhill. It's hard to hold these things together.

> How with this rage shall beauty hold a plea
> Whose action is no stronger than a flower?
> O! how shall summer's honey breath hold out,
> Against the wrackful siege of batt'ring days?

Shakespeare's words had been haunting me since the Manchester bombing, and now this. Was the frailty of poetry, the gossamer web of vision, simply to be blown away by these battering days?

Somehow the opposite happened: beauty's action, in every blossom, in every gesture of grace, seemed stronger than ever. The rage in me surged and went.

In the morning, when, the cathedral still out of bounds, I checked my phone to see what route I might take home, I saw the blocked ways: the bridge, Borough High Street, the Thames-side roads to left and right, picked out on the screen in red, forming a distinct cross, a cross at whose heart was the hurt, and I remembered Traherne's lovely words to Christ: 'I will not by the noise of bloody wars and the dethroning of kings advance you to glory: but by the gentle ways of peace and love.'

7

In a Railway Carriage

Other people's conversation in railway carriages – you just can't help overhearing it. Or so I tell myself.

I was on the train from Leicester to Cambridge, on a hot June day, listening to the conversation between three people sitting around the table opposite me, two men talking earnestly to one another about trains. Beside one was a woman, his wife, I think, trying, just occasionally, to broaden the conversation.

The men's talk was both technical and enthusiastic. Indeed, the more technical it was, the more enthusiastic it became. Details of track-gauges, name-plates, the maintenance history of certain steam engines, an exact recall of particular engine numbers, and, above all, the specifics, the precise details, of railway time-tables.

I discerned there must be a poetry in this obsession with completing lists of times, dates, and engine numbers; a poetry of detail, completion, and inclusion. But I confess that, as the conversation wore on, the poetry of it began to elude me.

What stopped their flow was that the train itself stopped at the little station at Manea. I had never known a train stop there before. Even our small four-coacher was longer than the bare platform where we idled in the sunlight. No one left and no one came. And then the woman, taking advantage of a pause in the flow of the men's conversation, changed everything with just one word. She looked around and said, as if into the air: 'Adlestrop!'

Suddenly we were all on another train, more than 100 years ago, as the steam hissed at its halt that other June day, in the summer before the Great War, and the poet Edward Thomas, so soon to die in the trenches, looked out at the empty platform and saw the name:

> ... Adlestrop – only the name
> And willows, willow-herb, and grass,
> And meadowsweet, and haycocks dry,
> No whit less still and lonely fair
> Than the high cloudlets in the sky.

That name, as the woman spoke it now, summoned the whole poem, and somehow we, too, through the clear air of this Cambridgeshire fenland, also heard, as Edward Thomas did:

> ... mistier,
> Farther and farther, all the birds
> Of Oxfordshire and Gloucestershire.

Both men turned to the woman, and I could see that they knew the poem, as I did, and perhaps other people in the carriage did, too. In this particular place and time we suddenly came to a sense of something more, a sense of the whole, just as, for Edward Thomas, one blackbird had somehow summoned all the birds.

Or so I was thinking, when the train jerked into motion again and one of the men leant forward and said excitedly to his friend: 'Actually they've worked out the timetable for that exact train. Yes, I've got the details here: 24 June 1914. I've not got the specific engine number yet, but it would have got into Adlestrop at precisely 12.45 ...'

I exchanged a brief glance with the woman as, each in our

own way, we settled back to inhabit the different poetries of our common journey.

8

In the Margins

BLISS. I have escaped for three days to the book-lined walls, the intricately carved wooden galleries, and the civilized calm of Gladstone's Library in Hawarden.

For a bibliophile, it doesn't get better than this: a library you live in, where the magic password of your room number lets you take your book and drift into the spacious common room, all worn leather sofas, old chessboards, and whisky from the honesty bar; or into the library's own nooks and crannies and special-collections rooms, where you curl up with your prize and read, read, read, uninterrupted and guilt-free.

All the books are on shelves or in presses, nothing in a vault; so browsing is an indulgence and an inspiration. Every distraction turns out to be a crucial clue, something you should have read in the first place.

At the core of the collection are the Grand Old Man's own books, brought down from the castle in wheelbarrows by that august personage himself. And in his books are his annotations and underlinings, his fascinating marginalia.

Today I held in my hand Gladstone's copy of Hallam Tennyson's memoir of his father, the poet. Gladstone has heavily marked and annotated Hallam's account of how Tennyson wrote *In Memoriam*, the beautiful poem in memory of his namesake Arthur Henry Hallam, the young man whom Gladstone and Tennyson both loved so dearly. It's a poem I love, too, and it's still the best guide through doubt and grief.

The page fell open at a passage where Tennyson's son writes about his father's last days: 'A week before his death I was sitting with him and he talked … of the love of God, that God whose eyes consider the poor, who catereth even for the sparrow. "I should", he said, "infinitely rather feel myself the most miserable wretch on the face of the earth with a God above, than the highest type of man standing alone."'

Tracing the exclamations pencilled in the margins of this passage in Gladstone's own strong hand, I felt our physical and spiritual links as I held the book that bound so many loves together.

But it's not just in these great libraries that such connections live and kindle. How much of our own lives and passions are somehow bodied forth in the rubbed pages, worn bookmarks, and pencilled marginalia of our shared books!

And there is more; for we ourselves are living volumes, unfinished; and we write on one another's pages, sometimes tentative marginalia, sometimes heartfelt appeals across the main text.

Browsing this paradisaical library on the margins of Wales, I remembered the words of John Donne's 17th meditation – words of hope for the day when the broken texts of our lives will be translated at last into the language of heaven:

'God's hand is in every translation, and his hand shall bind up all our scattered leaves again for that library where every book shall lie open to one another.'

9

On the Lady Bridge

In the hot weather, one is glad of even the smallest glimpse of water. The cool clear stream of the Granta is especially attractive; so I lingered on the Lady Bridge and gazed awhile at the river.

> Willows whiten, aspens quiver,
> Little breezes dusk and shiver
> Thro' the wave that runs for ever …

Tennyson's lines rippled through my mind, and there did, indeed, come one of those little breezes for which one is so grateful. As the ripples came and went, the reflections in the water – the trees, the bridge, myself leaning on the rail – dissolved and recomposed, dissolved and recomposed. I wondered whether the sudden fluctuations in political fortune which we have witnessed of late, compelling, dramatic, important as they are in one sense, might also, in another sense, be no more than ripples on the surface of something deeper.

Suddenly, a bigger circle of ripples broke my reflection again, and I looked up to see Mussolini strutting, splashing, and generally disporting himself in the shallow waters.

I should, perhaps, mention that Mussolini is the local name for a fat white goose who can often be seen throwing his weight around and attempting to lord it over the more modestly proportioned ducks and ducklings in the river. He does them no harm, of course, and they seem unperturbed – however alarmed the ducklings may be at first. They soon learn from their mothers to pay no attention, and Mussolini's fantasies of river domination, if he has them, get no further than his own little skull.

There's something about his pompous gait that is intrinsically ridiculous, and everyone (Mussolini excepted) seems to know it. If only one might have said the same for his namesake; if only it had been sufficient for a few of the village girls to say 'Oh, you silly goose' to put a stop to that goose-stepping, too. But, somehow, the human strutters and pretenders among us contrive to be taken more seriously.

I was roused from these reflections by the sound of a bell ringing out from the high church tower of St Mary the Virgin, where it shimmered in the heat. The Lady Bridge takes its name, like the church to which it leads, from that other village girl, who sang a song to her cousin up in the hill country, a song that says everything that needs to be said to the Mussolinis of this world, past, present, and future.

The bell sounded and trembled once more through the still air, and I found myself longing for the cool shade and deep silence that awaited me in the ancient church. Soon, our morning hymn floated out over the surface of that silence:

As pants the hart for cooling streams
When heated in the chase,
So longs my soul, O God, for thee,
And thy refreshing grace.

10

Two Clocks

We have come again to that time of year when the banks and shoals of visitors to Cambridge swirl and veer down King's Parade, and brave tour guides, bearing flags on long poles above the swaying heads, wade through the thick of them, trying to gather their respective groups around them and hustle them from one college to the next.

An extra hazard for the last of the students riding through on their cycles is the knot and cluster of tourists who gather in the middle of the road at the junction of King's Parade and Bene't Street to stare at Corpus Christi's weirdly beautiful Chronophage clock and, in particular, at the hideous locust perched above it, which is constantly, as its name suggests, eating time.

I was there in 2008 when it was unveiled by the man who has penetrated the mystery of time more deeply than most, Stephen Hawking. I remember when the veil came away and I first saw the golden circles turning, and, above them, the dark locust, which appears to devour the minutes but is in fact the clock's escapement mechanism, displayed and functioning on the outside rather than the interior.

For the Chronophage, time is constantly consumed. It sees 'our minutes hasten to their end'. It measures only 'the years that the locust hath eaten'. And I suppose, recollecting it now, I should think fearfully of all the minutes that it has consumed since I stood there nine years ago, sipping a glass of wine

31

whose richness and depth was also the gift of time, and trying, in vain, to understand Professor Hawking's opening remarks.

But I beg to differ with the Chronophage. Yes, time is fleeting, but it is also constantly renewed, and, for every moment that is taken from us, another is given, pristine and beautiful.

So, in my mind's eye, I have set up another timepiece, a counter-clock to Corpus Christi's Chronophage. Like the Chronophage, my imaginary clock turns in beautiful golden circles; like the Chronophage, it takes its motion from a point beyond itself; but, in my clock, time is not being clawed back and consumed: it is being poured out liberally and constantly renewed; for the figure above the golden circles in my clock is not a ravenous locust, but an angel of God, taking the riches of eternity and pouring them out moment by moment into the circles of time.

Such was the vision of Dante, who saw time and motion as ultimately given and renewed by Divine Love, by what he called, in the last line of his great poem, 'the Love that moves the sun and the other stars'.

We might christen my clock a Chronodor, a time-*giver*. It would witness to God's promise, in the book of Joel: 'I will restore to you the years that the locust hath eaten.'

The Corpus Chronophage cost a cool million; my Chronodor, like the gift of time which it celebrates, is completely free.

11

The Threshold of the New

The slow bus from Linton to Cambridge winds its way each morning through the little village of Abington. One of the pleasures of my commute in the past couple of weeks has been the chance to watch two thatchers at work, as we trundled past a cottage whose roof they were renewing.

Over that fortnight, I witnessed a miracle of gradual transformation: the dull grey of the old thatch gave way to golden reed, all freshly dressed and resplendent in the sun, until the whole was a new-made glory, shining like Heorot, the golden-roofed mead-hall of Hrothgar, which the Beowulf poet called

foremost of halls under heaven;
Its radiance shone over many lands.

Of course, this was no Saxon mead-hall but a little country cottage, and yet in the art of thatching there was continuity.

The thatchers themselves were fascinating. There was an older man, clearly the master craftsman and in charge: tall, wiry, tanned with sun and wind. He had a kind, wise face and longish silver hair, which I guessed must once have been as golden as the reeds he so skilfully pinned into place. The other was clearly his apprentice: a younger man with hair still bright as straw – perhaps, I wondered, his son. Here, too, in the passing of the craft to a new generation, was a continuity to be cherished.

From my window in the bus I could see the older man instructing his apprentice, but couldn't hear their conversation. I guessed, though, that some of those lovely old words, peculiar to thatching, were hanging for a moment in the Abington air, as he named their unique tools: the 'twisle', and the 'spragger', and showed his apprentice how to lift the 'nitch' and set the 'fleaking' right.

Relishing what Hopkins calls 'áll trádes, their gear and tackle and trim' might have led me into mere nostalgia for a bygone age; but that is not what thatching is for. Thatching is not about looking back: it's about making things new again: restoring the grey into gold, making things fast, watertight, and workable.

As I watched that grey-haired man transform and renew the roof on which he worked, I remembered, with sudden poignancy, those lovely lines of George Peele's:

His golden locks Time hath to silver turn'd
O Time too swift, O swiftness never ceasing ...

I thought how, in this world, the old cottage with its new thatch had outlasted many human lives, and would outlive the man who was renewing it now. But then Edmund Waller's last poem, 'Old Age', came to my mind unbidden:

The soul's dark cottage, battered and decayed
Lets in new light through chinks that time hath made ...

As the bus moved on, I looked back for one last glimpse of the thatchers, and Waller's last lines echoed in my mind:

Leaving the old, both worlds at once they view,
That stand upon the threshold of the new.

12

Transfiguration

Treasuring a little leisure in idle August, I lie on my back at the fringe of the wood on Rivey Hill, and look up at the shimmer of light through leaves, enjoying for a moment the very thing that Coleridge glimpsed in his lime-tree bower:

> Pale beneath the blaze
> Hung the transparent foliage; and I watch'd
> Some broad and sunny leaf, and lov'd to see
> The shadow of the leaf and stem above
> Dappling its sunshine!

Then the cloud comes back and it is gone; I stir my stumps and continue my walk. That little glimpse of translucence has set me in mind of this Sunday's feast of the transfiguration, a favourite for me. I'd climbed Linton's little hill and had my glimpse of light, but now I contemplated that other mountain, where the sudden radiance was not just a glimpse but a vision.

I love that story, just as I love the story of Moses and the burning bush. I like the truth they both disclose: that the divine presence does not annihilate what it meets, but transfigures and fulfils it.

The bush is not consumed, but stays as true and rooted in earth as ever, though now resplendent with heaven. And Moses, who gives it new attention, and feels at last, with unshod feet, God's holy ground, does not cease himself to be grounded or to see the common bush in front of him – only now he knows that nothing is common.

So, too, the divine nature does not do away with the ordinary body that Jesus shares with us, but on that mountain the veil is lifted and we see 'heaven in ordinary'. Somehow, I feel that the moment of the burning bush and the moment of transfiguration are the same moment: what is promised in one, 'I will come down', is fulfilled in the other. And in the gospel story, Moses is there to see it happen!

My own sonnet on the transfiguration opens with a sense of those moments in both testaments meeting:

> For that one moment in and out of time
> On that one mountain where all moments meet …

Certainly this feast is central for all painters and poets: 'Earth's crammed with heaven', Elizabeth Barrett Browning says. 'And every common bush afire with God, But only he who sees, takes off his shoes.'

It's the painters and poets who invite us to take off our shoes and open our eyes. So Herbert urges us not to 'stay … [our] eye' on the world's glassy surface, but 'through it pass and then the heav'n espy'.

We leave Mount Tabor with eyes newly opened:

> As fresh and pure as water from a well …
> The source of all our seeing rinsed and cleansed.

Edwin Muir's lovely lines on the transfiguration were also in my mind when, at the end of my sonnet, I imagined the disciples, amid the darkness of Good Friday, remembering that light:

> Nor can this blackened sky, this darkened scar
> Eclipse that glimpse of how things really are.

13

A Childhood Memory?

I am staying for a while with my mother up in Scotland. She is a hale and hearty 98, and she has just told me a remarkable story.

We were looking together at a book on Coleridge and his *Rime of the Ancient Mariner*, which I dedicated to her when I published it earlier this year. I was recalling how, when I was a child, in the days when we often used to be out at sea, among the few passengers on cargo ships plying their way between Southern Africa and England, she used to recite me passages from the *Ancient Mariner*, and that is how, when I could scarcely hold a book or read for myself, I came to know and love that poem.

It was the beginning of a lifelong fascination, for here we were in Scotland, more than half a century later, still chanting great chunks of the poem together.

But when we got to the lines 'At length did cross an albatross, Through the fog it came', my mother paused and said: 'Do you remember the albatross?'

'No,' I said, 'at least, I don't think so.'

'Oh,' she replied, 'we were rounding the Cape of Good Hope, out there where the Indian Ocean becomes the South Atlantic, and we were up on deck together. You would have been about six, and we saw far off the great white shape of an albatross flying. That was a rare sight in itself. But then, a rarer thing happened: it flew towards the ship and came and perched a moment, high on a rail above us, and looked at us with its bright eye, then spread its wide white wings and flew on.'

This was new to me, yet somehow, as my mother spoke, I could see it so clearly in my mind's eye: the pitching deck, the great green rolling waves, myself holding my mother's hand and above us the vast white bird. Was it my imagination inspired at once by Coleridge's poem and my mother's vivid recollection? Or had her words uncovered and renewed some buried memory, some image I had carried, caught in the tenacious networks of my mind, and suddenly released?

Could I remember back to that moment, as a little boy far out at sea, in the strange year of 1963? The year that Kennedy, and Aldous Huxley, and C. S. Lewis died on the same day.

Suddenly, linked in the intimacy of association to that image my mother had summoned, came another memory: a memory from a favourite childhood story, *The Voyage of the Dawn Treader*, a memory of the moment when Lucy, a little girl far out at sea, in darkness and dire straits, prays for help, and sees a beam of light, and, looking along the beam, sees a shape like a cross, and sees at last that it is a great white albatross! It flies close by her and speaks, in a familiar voice, the three words she needed then and I need now: 'Courage, dear heart.'

14

A Dry-stone Wall

There is something deeply satisfying about a well-made dry-stone wall. It is a single, beautiful, functional thing, and yet every part of it is different.

I was gazing the other day at one section of a wall bordering a path up into the Lomond hills in Fife, admiring the gentle gradation from the larger stones at the base to the smaller ones at the top, all held fast and stabilized by the big coping stones running down on either side. Each stone unique, yet all beautifully holding together, clenched and fastened by their own weight, by the very forces that, differently disposed, might have pulled them apart.

Even the gaps and spaces here and there were beautiful in shape. And the whole wall was figured and variegated by the blotch and mottle of weathering, decorated with lichen of many colours and tones, from strong yellows to delicate browns and filigree patterns of white.

Through, between, and over the stones there was new green growth: the mosses and grass growing back, not to reclaim the stone, for they had never lost it, but to bed it in, secure it further, make it more at home and naturally fitting in the place it was set. It was a sight at once restful and delightful to the eye, at once soothing and stimulating.

The phrase about someone 'staring at a brick wall' came into my mind, but this was no brick wall. This hand-made collage of variety and happenstance was the opposite of that machine-made uniformity.

Another phrase surfaced, this time from Pink Floyd's *The Wall*: 'All in all you're just another brick in the wall.' There is something darkly ambiguous in their having used a choir of schoolchildren to sing 'We don't need no education' in that song, but there is no doubt that they were right to protest against any process of formation or education that reduces our particular, individual, mottled humanity to 'just another brick', formed in a mould and cemented into place.

The old term 'edification' came also to mind, and I thought that, when it comes to being edified, being built up into something strong and worth while, a dry-stone wall might be a better metaphor for educators and pastors than a cemented brick one.

I remembered the words of St Peter, that awkward man whom Jesus fondly called a stone: 'Like living stones, let yourselves be built into a spiritual house.' I looked again at the beautiful wall in front of me, each stone, in its own particular shape, somehow accommodated to the whole, lifted up from its isolated place in the field, heaved and hefted, set into a new place for a new purpose, leaning on and yet supporting its neighbours.

Might I let myself be built, I wondered, and even as I walked on I began to feel the heft and heave, the strength that lifts, but also the skilful and tender touch of wounded hands on living stone.

15

Liturgical Moments

I love the way liturgy lifts the ordinary for a moment into the eternal, and everyday actions, so often automatic and unnoticed, coruscate in the divine light and are enacted with complete attention, full intention.

It is not only during the central acts of the Eucharist – the breaking of bread and pouring of wine, eating and drinking – that the daily veil that covers the sublime is lifted. Even an everyday handshake is elevated to something more in sharing the Peace, and smaller things, peripheral and unnoticed, are given the kiss of life with liturgy.

There is a verse or a prayer for putting on a stole, for washing one's hands, for preparing to leave the vestry and enter the church. I have friends who remember the scourging of Christ as they do up the buttons on their cassocks.

These moments of liturgical attention are the accretion of centuries, and I sometimes wonder how long it will be before some of the routines of contemporary church life are dignified with a verse from scripture and a moment of prayer, especially the routines that we all witness and often experience as interruption rather than prayer.

The clipping and unclipping of a radio microphone on to vestments. The awkward moment when a priest fumbles in his or her pocket for the switch to turn the microphone off for the singing of a hymn (this may be a genuine work of mercy). And then fumbles again to turn it on for the next collect.

Perhaps in 50 years or so there will be a new little vestry ritual: a versicle and response for the verger as they switch on the sound system. I amuse myself in odd moments wondering what those versicles and responses might be; for the Scriptures (especially in the Authorized Version) are replete with possibilities.

For putting the rechargeable battery back in its charger:

> V: They that wait upon the Lord
>
> R: Shall renew their strength (Isaiah 40.31)

For clipping on of the microphone:

> V: I will magnify thee, O Lord
>
> R: For thou hast set me up (Psalm 30.1)

And for that discreet little fumble to turn the microphone on:

> V: Let not thy left hand know
>
> R: What thy right hand doeth (Matthew 6.5)

These idle fancies may never come to pass, but something better is already happening. For I have found that the discipline of mindfulness, of attention to the ordinary in liturgy, to taking, breaking, sharing, pouring, raising, drinking, has an effect that lasts through the week.

That full presence to what I am doing at the altar sometimes spills over, through and beyond the church doors, and I find myself more aware of the beauty and power of a gesture in the rest of the week: sharing food with a friend, pouring wine for a guest. Perhaps there is no need to add to the liturgy when the liturgy itself has helped me to find heaven in ordinary.

16

And Did Those Feet?

And did those feet in ancient time
Walk upon England's mountains green?

Probably not. But I was invited to indulge in just that specula-
tion when I took part in recording a radio programme about
Blake's 'Jerusalem'. Blake was alluding, of course, to the lovely
cycle of legends centred on Glastonbury, and particularly to
the story that Joseph of Arimathea, as a Phoenician trader,
had brought Jesus as a child to England when he came to buy
tin from the Cornish mines.

There was such a trade in New Testament times; so the
whole glorious story is theoretically possible, but we were
all agreed, on the programme, that it was very unlikely to
have happened, and, indeed, that the next part of the legend,
in which Joseph returns to England, after the resurrection,
bearing with him the holy grail, and plants his staff in the
English earth, where it roots and flowers in the Glastonbury
thorn, may also involve some wishful thinking.

With the one exception of an episode in the Temple in
Jerusalem, the Gospels are strangely silent on Jesus' childhood
and youth, and so it's natural for all of us who love him to try
and imagine those hidden years. It is also natural to imagine
Jesus in our own country, to picture him transfiguring some
familiar landscape.

There is truth in such imagination; for all Christians bear

Christ with them, and we walk our green hills in him and he in us. I have walked the wolds and folds of England with my friends and sensed his presence in our talk and in all we saw, walking together in faith.

Perhaps the real question is not about the 'ancient time', but about the present and the future. For Jesus comes to England not only in and with and through all of us who are christened, en-Christed, but surely also in the stranger, in the unknown figure who draws near us as we walk. The encounter on the road to Emmaus was not a one-off, but a sign of things to come.

> *And was the holy Lamb of God*
> *On England's pleasant pastures seen?*

Perhaps not in those days, but now the Lamb is here! The child Jesus may not have made the dangerous crossing from the Middle East to our green and pleasant land, but there are plenty of children who have done just that in the past few years. We need not look to the past, but only open our eyes to the present. Blake asks, in another place, that we should 'cleanse the doors of perception'. If we did, then we might well see, in the face of a child refugee, the Countenance Divine shining forth upon our clouded hills.

They asked us, on the radio programme, whether we would be singing along to 'Jerusalem' on the last night of the Proms, and I, for one, will be doing just that. But I will sing it, not as a jingoistic song for little England, but as an anthem of renewed vision, the vision of a heavenly Jerusalem, whose name means 'city of peace'.

17

Gazing at Hodge

I stood the other day, gazing through the window of a house in the City of London, at the statue of a cat.

This was no ordinary cat; for the statue commemorated Samuel Johnson's cat, Hodge, whom Doctor Johnson famously described as 'a very fine cat indeed', for whose sake he used to hasten to Billingsgate market to buy oysters, because his manservant was too ashamed to be seen in public buying the trashy food of the poor. But Hodge liked oysters, and Johnson took pleasure in his pleasure. For the house through whose window I gazed was 17 Gough Square, one of the great shrines of England: the house in which Johnson compiled his incomparable dictionary. It gave me as much pleasure to stand there as eating the oysters must have given Hodge.

Of course, a good book 'makes one little room an everywhere', and I can pull out my dog-eared pocket Boswell in the corner of any railway carriage and find myself at once ensconced at the Mitre, while the good Doctor discourses with Goldsmith and Burke over the Madeira, and his little Scottish friend takes notes.

But there is still something special about being in a great writer's house, about climbing the same foot-worn stairs, admiring the same pictures, looking through the same window. And, in Johnson's house, they keep a copy of the dictionary lying open on the table. You can turn its pages in the very room where it was compiled.

There is another, and, for me, deeper and more personal aura about that house. It was here, too, in the midst of all that he achieved, that Johnson encountered, suffered, and resisted his terrible bouts of depression – those visitations of 'the black dog', a phrase that Johnson used in a letter to a friend and bequeathed to Churchill, who made it famous.

Johnson was sometimes paralysed and speechless with his depression, unwilling and, indeed, unable to see friends: a double blow for a man to whom eloquence and friendship were among life's greatest joys. Even though his melancholy sometimes put on a quasi-religious garb, it was, in fact, Johnson's deep faith that sustained him and helped him through.

It used to trouble me that the statue of Johnson, just round the corner, outside St Clement Danes, is placed so that the great man has his back to the church. But now I am glad of it. Now I see that, in a modern phrase Johnson would have relished, Jesus could say to Johnson: 'I've got your back; you can advance.'

The faith that sustained Johnson enabled him to step out from the church to face and engage the world. He looks down towards Fleet Street, to where the words of the worldly were waiting to be challenged and renewed by the words of a man who was himself renewed and sustained by the Word.

And, when Johnson finally got home, I fancy that the black dog was sometimes kept at bay by a very fine black cat.

18

Septembral

September has a special feel. The light and leisure of August lingers into it a little, and yet it is also somehow brisk and exciting, quickened with promise, with endings and renewings: the start of terms and all the other turnings of the year. It carries the plumped fullness of harvest, but also breathes a clean new scent, a change in the wind.

I was especially glad, therefore, when I came upon the word 'Septembral'. It seemed right and fitting that September should have its own adjective. I found the word in some lines of Hilaire Belloc's 'Heroic Poem in Praise of Wine':

> The years dissolve. I am standing in that hour
> Of majesty Septembral, and the power
> Which swells the clusters when the nights are still
> With autumn stars on Orvieto hill.

These lines were all the more poignant for me, since I, too, had seen the stars from Orvieto hill, and his Septembral remembering kindled mine.

It's likely that Belloc borrowed the word from his beloved Rabelais who wrote, after a truly Rabelaisian drinking bout: 'My head aches a little, and I perceive that the registers of my brain are somewhat jumbled and disordered with the Septembral juice.'

Belloc and Rabelais were both praising wine, but here the

real Septembral juice is cider, and the glory of September in England shines and oozes from her apples. My college has wonderful old apple orchards bearing unique varieties, with names such as Peasgood's Nonesuch and Norfolk Beefing. In late September, their branches are laden with red and gold, ready to offer new students an orgy of delicious scrumping.

Before those students arrive, I'll have time to savour September in our orchards and call to mind the most truly Septembral poet of all, remembering that other September in 1819, when Keats seemed to glimpse Autumn herself, as she began

> ... to load and bless
> With fruit the vines that round the thatch eves run,
> To bend with apples the mossed cottage trees.
> And fill all fruit with ripeness to the core.

As September ends, and the students return, some of the new ones will ask me what they should go and see in Cambridge. Rather than send them to the big monuments and famous colleges, I'll direct them to a little gallery in the Fitzwilliam Museum where they can lift a brown cover from a display case and see Samuel Palmer's most perfect picture: *The Magic Apple Tree*. In that painting, an Edenic and unfallen light briefly transfigures the little village of Shoreham.

Palmer's 'Valley of Vision' – the apple tree, the fields of grain, and the church spire – offer a concentrated beauty, which at once affirms and transcends the world. He was Blake's disciple, but for Palmer the spire of the parish church, which marks the very centre of his painting, was not the mark of the oppressor as it might have been for Blake, but the very place through which all that Septembral glory might tremble at last into praise.

19

The Namer and the Named

In my peregrinations round Britain over the past few months, I have carried with me Robert Macfarlane's stimulating book *Landmarks*.

Macfarlane explores the rich word-hoard that links landscape and language. From waterlands to woodlands, edgelands to earthlands, he unearths the earthiest, the most embodied and particular, words with which we have sought to name and know, shape and reshape, imagine and reimagine the woods and waters among which we live. The glossaries that accompany each section of the book are a joy in themselves.

Macfarlane's contention is that naming nature – its features, its sounds, its minute particulars – enables us to know and appreciate it in new ways, and also initiates both namer and named into a kind of covenantal, almost sacral relationship, making it less likely that we will trash or degrade the world around us.

Certainly, his book has clarified, and fine-tuned, my awareness of place, my appreciation of where I am, and how I am compassed about by life and beauty. But it has also brought me to the brink of language, as much as to the brinks and edges of landscape.

As I stood on the brink of a burn that flows by my uncle's old croft in the wilds of Wester Ross, I listened to the water rush and fall over stone and under heather, and felt that it was both spilling and spelling itself, that there was a kind of speech

– indeed, a kind of poetry – in its mellifluous sounds.

Macfarlane's book had given me some wonderful new words to apprehend that sound: *threeple* and *tripple*, Cumbrian dialect words for 'the gentle sound made by a quick-flowing stream'; and, from Scots dialect, *jabble,* for 'the agitated movement of water; a splashing and dashing in small waves or ripples'.

But, even with Macfarlane's help, I could not really spell or capture what I heard the burn singing; its utterance was just upstream of human language.

Coleridge, who loved and beautifully described the welling and movement of streams and waterfalls, came to my mind. A lively passage from one of his letters comes closer than I ever could to what I heard and saw: 'What a sight it is to look down on such a Cataract! – the wheels, that circumvolve in it – the leaping up & plunging forward of that infinity of Pearls & Glass Bulbs – the continual *change* of the *Matter*, the perpetual *sameness* of the *form* – it is an awful image & Shadow of God & the World.'

I can never find language entirely adequate to the beauty and particularity of the world around me, but Coleridge also comforts me with a radical thought. He reverses the flow and makes me see that I am not just the namer, but also the named. For Coleridge, the whole world, and all of us within it, are not just objects, but are also an utterance. We are words from the Word, as he speaks us into being:

> The lovely shapes and sounds intelligible
> Of that eternal language, which thy God
> Utters.

20

House for Duty

I wrote recently that autumn was a season of change and renewal. Well, change and renewal arrived in the form of two svelte and lithe-limbed newcomers taking up residence with us in the rectory at Linton.

George and Zara have come to us from the Retired Greyhounds Trust. Perhaps they have been sent to give us a foretaste of what retirement might be like, though they are in no way retiring, but, on the contrary, affectionate, eager to please, and, even when stretched across the couch in a post-walk stupor, impossibly elegant.

Though they have retired from racing, it would be fairer to say that, like some other retired wearers of a dog collar, they have taken up 'house for duty'. But, unlike many clergy, their duty is genuinely light: all they need do – and they do it daily and delightfully – is lead me out and lift my spirits.

This autumnal transition has been a long time coming. This time last year, as I pushed myself to walk the paths and cross the little bridges, the fords and fields and woodlands around Linton, I was holding grief on an invisible lead, walking a golden absence, my footsteps dogged only by a memory; for we had lost Paddy, our golden Labrador.

Wherever I turned on the old paths, and especially when I met the other dog-walkers, I would half glimpse what was not there. But, after a long winter and the renewals of spring and summer, Maggie and I sensed that it was time to open our doors again; and, having made the acquaintance of these two hounds in need of a home, we knew we had the home to offer.

They really are remarkable creatures. There is something archaic, almost heraldic, about a greyhound. They look as if they've just stepped out of a medieval illumination; they would blend into the Bayeux tapestry. Those loose limbs, slender waists, long necks, and keen noses seem unchanged since the hieroglyphs of Egypt; and yet here is a brace of them with their heads in my lap, as I sit musing in my cluttered study.

We have still to make each other's acquaintance properly and deeply, but already I am wondering what they will teach me. To sense a little more and linger a little longer on my walks, certainly, and to relax a little more deeply when I come home and close the door.

A Dominican friend of mine, striking in his white habit and black cloak, explained to me once that the heraldic greyhound holding a torch in its mouth on the cover of the *New Blackfriars* journal was really a pun: the *Dominicani,* Dominicans, were also the *Domini Cani,* the dogs of God, happy to walk for him in the world, and keen to scent the truth.

As it happens, George, in white with black markings, and Zara, glossy black with a white diamond, put me in mind of that habit. I feel sure that they will indeed be Domini Cani to all of us at the rectory.

21

A Flock of Words

I took part in a service in Ely Cathedral recently. Three different poets had been invited to reflect with the evening congregation on poetry and the environment.

While one of the poets was reading, a remarkable thing happened. She was reciting to us a beautiful and thought-provoking poem that invited us to imagine human life from the perspective of a bird soaring above us and, puzzling over our slow, earth-bound, convoluted struggles, calling us to tread on the earth more lightly.

As she read, we were suddenly aware of a fluttering whirr and whisper of wings, as a wood pigeon launched herself from a high ledge, and circled out above us in the wide and sacred space beneath the cathedral's famous lantern, almost as though she had been summoned by the poem.

The poet, quite rightly, paused, and let the bird play her part in our worship and reflection, lifting us unexpectedly into another region.

I'm recalling that moment now, around Francis-tide, when churches might be opened more intentionally to birds and animals. Indeed, I once preached in Ely on St Francis's Day to a congregation that consisted not only of people and their pets, but of several thousand bees, brought in their glass-sided hive for the occasion.

The feast of St Francis always brings to my mind Seamus Heaney's fine early poem 'Saint Francis and The Birds', where he says:

> When Francis preached love to the birds
> They listened, fluttered, throttled up
> Into the blue like a flock of words
> Released for fun from his holy lips.

Those lines give me a great deal to delight in, but especially that image of the birds themselves as a flock of words released for fun. It strikes me that this is both a helpful image of preaching and, perhaps more profoundly, of creation.

There is always a danger that any preacher's words will fall like lead: weighty words, lifted with great labour from solid commentaries, carried assiduously up the pulpit steps, and then dropped from a great height, with seriousness and gravitas, on the heads of an unsuspecting congregation.

What fun to think of them, instead, as a flock of birds, alive and feathered, exploring an open space, wheeling and pirouetting, landing, perhaps, and nesting in the dry branches of those weary souls that need them most!

And, even when the readings call for something darker and more dense, a good sermon might still lift into the open, darken, shift, and shiver, like a dense throng of starlings, all flying freely, and yet somehow bound together; a mysterious murmuration, summoning new shapes and patterns against October's stormy skies.

Heaney's lines hint at creation, too. Francis released words from his holy lips, but his Lord, the Living Word, speaks the whole creation into being.

Perhaps all the birds that dance on the wing through our

world have been released for fun from the holy lips of our Maker, just like the one that helped a poet's words take flight in Ely Cathedral.

22

Autumn Leaves

As autumn deepens from September into October, it makes a transition from Keats to Shelley: from the 'season of mists and mellow fruitfulness' to the 'wild West Wind, thou breath of Autumn's being'; from the 'half-reap'd furrow...Drows'd with the fume of poppies', to the leaves

> ... driven, like ghosts from an enchanter fleeing,
> Yellow, and black, and pale, and hectic red...

The sound of wind in the trees always stirs me, and the beauty of the leaves themselves, as lovely when they fall as when they stay, is always a revelation.

The start of the Michaelmas term moves me too, and drew from me the opening of my Michaelmas sonnet in *Sounding the Seasons*:

> Michaelmas gales assail the waning year,
> And Michael's scale is true, his blade is bright.
> He strips dead leaves, and leaves the living clear
> To flourish in the touch and reach of light.

Such stripping away is always clarifying, always a call to renewal. As autumn reveals the underlying pattern of bare branches, once veiled in summer green, it also reveals other patterns: the roots and branches of a faith that stays when our other flourishings fade and fail.

If there is a beauty in the leaves as they fly and fall, there is a beauty, too, in the new patterns that they make when they come to rest; when they are layered and, in every sense, interleaved, overlaying one another like the layers of memory as they gather and deepen, season by season.

From my window in college, I can see this year's freshers scrunching through the leaves with new-found friends, or setting off on their cycles against the freshening wind, their hair (and occasionally stray leaves of their essays) streaming out behind them, and I remember my own time as a fresher here – though the layers and leaves of memory between that time and this lie 40 autumns thick.

I still have some lines that I wrote back then, in a poem about leave-taking. I read them now as a note from my 20-year-old self to the man turning 60, about what he will remember:

> And if you leave, I leave, you leave me these
> These leaves of memory so thickly falling,
> Flame-coloured, floating slowly from the trees
> Through dappled light and into shadows drifting,
> Becoming earth, decaying by degrees
> To loam-deep stillness we will keep at parting.

There is this difference, though, between my remembering then and now; for now I have a faith that memory is not only about parting. Now, I know that there is a kind of remembering which is, in every sense, re-membering: putting back together the lost and broken – a remembering that is not about loss and absence, but about renewal and presence.

And, as I make my way through this year's fallen leaves to the chapel where I will celebrate the Eucharist, I know that, together with the breaking of bread and the sharing of wine, it will also be all my own remembering that I do in remembrance of him, and offer back for redemption and renewal.

23

An Emblem

The other day, I stepped from the noise and hurry of Fleet Street, its rushing cars, the unrelenting modernity of its steel and glass offices, and its stream of anxious, over-driven office workers, into the cool, beautiful interior, the space, grace, and calm of St Bride's.

It was as though I'd stepped into an oasis.

I was there to read my sonnet on the parable of the sower at a harvest thanksgiving.

Why St Bride's? The journalists' church is surely more associated with the pen than the plough. But this was the harvest service of the British Guild of Agricultural Journalists.

I was delighted to know that such a guild exists, and flourishes, for soon the church began to fill with a great throng of people whose care is to write about, and for, farmers, those for whom harvest is more than a quaint occasion for displaying one's apple-arranging skills.

It was clear from the sermon and prayers, and from the speeches at the lunch afterwards, that this was a guild of people deeply aware of the wider world around them, informed and concerned about global poverty, climate change, and the need for a renewed way of living on and with the land, reducing waste, recycling, moving towards a circular economy.

But what struck me most was their emblem, embossed on the order of service: a golden quill and a golden ear of wheat, crossed on a green ground. Obviously, it was well suited to their particular avocation, but it seemed to me that it was an apt emblem of my own vocation, too. From Homer to Heaney, poets have sensed a kinship between the lines of their verse and the long furrows opened by the plough: 'Each verse returning like the plough turned round.'

Poets know that their art also involves the sowing of seeds, the patient wait for growth, the need to weed out the extraneous, the art of discerning when a poem, like a crop, is ripe and ready.

But the guild's lovely emblem might be even more apt for the Christian poet. I remembered something that Micheal O'Siadhail once said when he was asked whether, as a Christian poet, he thought that his poems might sow the gospel seed.

'Oh, goodness, no,' he replied. 'In that parable, it is Christ who is both the sower and the seed. But I do notice how much attention Jesus pays to the soil itself, to whether and where the ground is good, and what makes it so. Just as I turn over my garden soil and shake it in a griddle to make it more kindly to the seed, so I hope that poetry might jostle the soil of the imagination, so that, when the sower goes out to sow, the seed might fall on good ground.'

His words were in my mind as I let the last words of my own sonnet sound out through St Bride's:

> O break me open, Jesus, set me free,
> Then find and keep your own good ground in me.

24

Gratitude

Browsing bookstalls is one of life's great pleasures. Like fishing, it remains a pleasure even if one brings nothing home; but today I had found a real treasure, and at a bargain price.

I stepped into the Eagle to order a celebratory pint and to leaf through my find at leisure. I was a little shocked at the price of the pint, but all that was set aside when I sat down to examine my new book. It was an odd volume from a little leather-bound set of the original *Spectator*, the collection of reflective essays which Joseph Addison and Richard Steele published as an ephemeral daily paper from 1711 to 1712, but which proved to be so popular and ground-breaking that it was collected and reprinted many times over for the rest of that century and beyond.

Indeed, the volume I held in my hand was printed and bound in 1747, but the bookseller had pencilled in 'odd volume – incomplete' and marked it down to £4! Of course, the fact that it was an odd volume made no odds at all, since each essay is complete in itself – it's not as if one were missing the climax of a three-decker novel – but it meant that I had in my hand a beautiful book, its lovely old pages bound and printed two decades before America was even a country, its fine font as elegant and readable now as then, and all for less than the price of my pint.

Compared with any other 'antiques', old books must be the best value of all.

As I turned the pages, I had another reason to be grateful for my find. My eye fell on 'No. 453 Saturday August 9th 1712', an essay by Addison which opens: 'There is not a more pleasing exercise of the mind than gratitude.' And soon the little essay flowers into verse:

When all thy mercies, O my God,
My rising soul surveys,
Transported with the view, I'm lost
In wonder, love, and praise.

So here was the source of a favourite hymn. That opening verse is especially dear to me, as it is the hymn that Maggie chose for her walk up the aisle on our wedding day, and those words were on my lips as I turned around to look at her.

And here, in their original context, were many other verses, more than those we sing: 13 in all. I had always liked the one about 'the slippery paths of youth', about Providence sustaining us even then, and how God's tender care is bestowed upon the child through the mother. But now I saw that Addison traces that care even further upstream:

Thy Providence my life sustained,
And all my wants redressed,
While in the silent womb I lay,
And hung upon the breast.

Certainly something to ponder in our own times. I was absorbed for a good hour in perusing this and other essays, and closed the book knowing that one more gift had been added to Addison's 'ten thousand':

Ten thousand thousand precious gifts
My daily thanks employ;
Nor is the least a cheerful heart,
That tastes those gifts with joy.

25

Hallowe'en

Hallowe'en approaches, and, as always, I have mixed feelings. I was blissfully unaware of this festival until we moved to Canada when I was ten, where Hallowe'en turned out to be quite a big thing. Its weird mixture of creepiness and candy troubled me, but, as a ten-year-old boy, I was prepared to put up with the creepiness for the sake of the candy, and went out trick-or-treating with all the rest.

Gradually, though, I found that the quotient of creepiness crept up, or perhaps I had less of a sweet tooth, and I was glad to leave it behind when I returned to England.

At least, I thought I'd left it behind.

For Hallowe'en seems to be creeping up again, creeping up on Christmas in the crass commercialism stakes, even here where the tradition is less strong. Now I know (though I didn't then) that Hallowe'en itself simply means the eve of All Hallows, the Christian feast of All Saints, a day when we think particularly of those souls in bliss who, even in this life, kindled a light for us, or, to speak more exactly, reflected for us and to us the already kindled light of Christ.

It's good that we should have a season of the year for remembrance, a time when we feel that the veil between time and eternity is thin, and we can sense that greater and wider communion of saints to which we belong. I am glad that the Church settled this feast on a time in the turning of the year when the pre-Christian Celtic religions were accustomed to think of and make offerings for the dead. The Church kept the day, but it changed the custom.

The greatest and only offering, to redeem both the living and the dead, has already been made by Christ, and if we want to celebrate our loving connections on both sides of the veil we need only now make gifts to the living, as we do in offering sweets to the trick-or-treaters in this season, and, far more profoundly, in exchanging gifts at Christmas.

I lament that both these seasons of hospitality and exchange have been wrenched from their first purpose to sell tinsel and sweeties; so I thought I might redress the balance a little with this sonnet for All Hallows, recalling the light that shines in darkness, who first kindled it, and how the saints reflect it.

Though Satan breaks our dark glass into shards
Each shard still shines with Christ's reflected light,
It glances from the eyes, kindles the words
Of all his unknown saints. The dark is bright
With quiet lives and steady lights undimmed,
The witness of the ones we shunned and shamed.
Plain in our sight and far beyond our seeing
He weaves them with us in the web of being.
They stand beside us even as we grieve,
The lone and left behind whom no one claimed,
Unnumbered multitudes, he lifts above
The shadow of the gibbet and the grave,
To triumph where all saints are known and named;
The gathered glories of his wounded love.

26

A Kingfisher

I was strolling early this morning with my two greyhounds, George and Zara, along Kingfisher Walk – a path that winds its way between a modern housing estate and a sinuous, high-banked, green-arched stretch of the Granta – when a sudden flash of dazzling electric blue, and a shimmering shape skimming at speed above the purls and turns of the water, announced that the kingfisher himself had graced us with his presence.

There is something all-transforming about the sudden appearance of such a bird, as though a veil has been lifted: for a moment, everything else is more beautiful, too; a familiar path has new possibilities.

For I had walked this path over the course of a year with no sighting, and had begun to fear that it was 'Kingfisher Walk' in name only, that, like all those suburban cul-de-sacs called 'Bluebell Wood' and 'Badgers' Sett', it was named after the very thing it had destroyed.

But here was the kingfisher taking possession of his domain again, as though his name alone had summoned him. Indeed, some words of summoning came immediately to my mind; for I had been revelling in Jackie Morris and Robert Macfarlane's magical new work *The Lost Words: A Spell Book*.

Macfarlane wrote a famous article some years ago lamenting that *The Oxford Junior Dictionary* had excised from its pages a whole cluster of words for English nature, as no longer used by modern children, words such as *acorn, bluebell, conker, dandelion, fern, heather, heron, and kingfisher.* Now he has made a spell book inviting children and adults to use these words again, and summon back all they have lost. His summoning spell for the kingfisher begins: 'Kingfisher: the colour-giver, fire-bringer, flame-flicker, river's quiver.' And those words were on my lips even as the kingfisher flickered upstream.

Macfarlane is a worthy successor to those other poets for whom the kingfisher's sudden presence was transformative: from Hopkins' 'As kingfishers catch fire, dragonflies draw flame'; to Heaney, meandering on the banks of the Moyola

Recalling the river's long swerve,
A kingfisher's blue bolt at dusk.

But my own sudden kingfisher summoned more than Macfarlane's summoning spell. It summoned a memory from years ago when I floated on this same river, a little further downstream, in an old wooden canoe, paddling out from Cambridge and up towards Grantchester, trying, with each stroke, to leave behind me a little of the fret and anxiety I had been absorbing as a chaplain.

Suddenly, a kingfisher flitted ahead of me, skimming the water with its ethereal blue, summoning me forward. I thought that was it, a single instant of blessing, but the bird waited and as I came up it skimmed forward again. Three times it glanced and skimmed ahead, like the robin in Narnia leading the children to adventure. By the time I came to Grantchester, and pulled out my canoe on the meadows by the Green Man, I was myself another man, blessed and charmed by the bird that Macfarlane calls:

Evening angler, weather-teller, rainbringer and
Rainbow bird – that sets the stream alight with burn and
glitter.

27

Health and Safety

I was in the charming cathedral city of Wells the other week when I had an interesting avian encounter. It was not the one I expected: with the swans who famously ring a bell on the moated wall of the Bishop's Palace to summon the staff when they want to be fed. I expect the Bishop of Bath and Wells is, like the Pope, a servant of the servants of God – but he is also a servant of these aristocratic swans. I was in Wells, however, to speak about Coleridge, and my encounter was with an albatross.

It turns out that the Wells and Mendip Museum has a fine display dedicated to *The Rime of the Ancient Mariner*, and to Coleridge as a local West Country writer. The display includes extracts from the accounts of Cook's voyages which influenced the poet's account of the albatross, some wonderful illustrations by Doré and others, and, surprisingly, an actual albatross, stuffed by a Victorian collector and gazing out at you from its tall glass case.

I was speaking at the Wells Festival of Literature, which takes place in a great white marquee on the other side of the moat, in the Bishop's Palace gardens, and the organisers told me that they had obtained permission to bring the albatross over from the museum so that it might sit opposite me on stage as I retold the mariner's tale. It was not to be.

For now the storm-blast came, and he
Was tyrannous and strong.

The last gales of Storm Brian had been flinging themselves on the little city. Just like the storm in the *Mariner*, Brian 'struck with his o'ertaking wings', and wuthered around us till the whole tent flapped and crackled and lunged in the gusts. The tent stayed grounded, however, and I was able to give my talk with added sound-effects; but, at the last minute, I was told that the museum had some concerns about health and safety, and had determined that moving the albatross in its fragile case across the green in these high winds might cause the glass to shatter and imperil not only the great bird itself, but also the good people of Wells.

It turns out that these specimens of the Victorian taxidermists' art cannot be exposed to the air because they contain the spores and germs of various diseases, which we, in a different century, might not be able to resist. So, holding the audience with my glittering eye as best I could, I carried on albatrossless.

Afterwards, the museum's honorary librarian kindly invited me to come and see what I had missed. As I gazed at this extraordinary bird, vaster than I could have imagined, and it gazed back with a sardonic, indeed ironic, expression, I couldn't help wondering what would have happened if the Mariner's vessel had been subject to a health-and-safety inspection before the voyage. With his cross-bow safely locked away below decks in a secure cabinet, there might have been no tale to tell, and one more albatross skimming the seas in freedom.

28

Raindrop

George and Zara, my two amiable greyhounds, continued their task of teaching me today. At their behest, we paused on our early-morning walk so that they might enjoy the rich *mélange* of scents which God was bringing to their noses. They were intensely present to the moment, quivering with excitement.

A human being can scarcely imagine how rich and various, how full of mystery and promise, must be the sensual experience of a dog nosing scents on a walk. It would be too much for us; we wouldn't have the maturity to cope, although Chesterton tried to imagine it in his 'The Song of Quoodle':

> The brilliant smell of water,
> The brave smell of a stone,
> The smell of dew and thunder,
> The old bones buried under …

But, as I paused with my dogs, my eye was caught by the gleam, the concentrated bead of light prismed in a single drop of the recent rain, still held in the valley-fold of a bent blade of grass, and I stooped to look at it more closely. I thought of Heaney's lovely lines at the end of 'Rainstick':

> You are like a rich man entering heaven
> Through the ear of a raindrop.

Those puzzling and beautiful words seemed a little clearer as I saw reflected back not only the light, but everything, made tiny and beautiful. Coleridge had a moment like that, too, and said in his Lay Sermon 'The Statesman's Manual' that he was 'struck with admiration at beholding the cope of heaven as imaged in a dew-drop'.

Suddenly, as is sometimes the way in the summoning chamber of my memory, I found that other poets were gathering around me to gaze on the same tiny bead of light. I heard Dylan Thomas urging me:

> [to] enter again the round
> Zion of the water bead
> And the synagogue of the ear of corn.

And behind him stood William Blake, reminding me

> To see a world in a grain of sand
> And a heaven in a wild flower,
> Hold infinity in the palm of your hand,
> And eternity in an hour.

I may envy George and Zara the finesse of their noses, I thought, but I do have this to intensify my experience: I have poetry. Coleridge called on poets to remove the 'film of familiarity', to 'awaken the mind's attention from the lethargy of custom, and direct it to the loveliness and the wonders of the world before us; an inexhaustible treasure for which we have eyes yet see not, ears that hear not and hearts that neither feel nor understand'.

The curved reflective surface of the drop, its dizzying changes of scale and perspective, had the effect of making it, as all poetry should be, both a mirror and a window. And, even as I thought this, one last poet seemed to join us: George Herbert. 'A man that looks on glass,' he said,

> On it may stay his eye;
> Or if he pleaseth, through it pass
> And then the Heav'n espy.

29

Can I Get There by Candlelight?

The curse of the White Witch on hapless Narnia was that it should be 'always winter and never Christmas'. The peculiarity of the Cambridge Michaelmas term is that it should be 'always Michaelmas and never Advent, let alone Christmas'.

For such is the timing of things that our final service of term, our Advent Carol Service, falls before Advent itself has even begun. Yet the college must somehow keep Christmas, and I don't want my students to follow the way of the world in losing sight of Advent altogether.

So I have decided that if Aslan could lift the witch's spell and breathe a midwinter spring into Narnia, strangely heralded by Father Christmas, then perhaps a college chaplain might also fold and refold Doctor Who's 'wibbly-wobbly, timey-wimey stuff', and bring in the season, even out of season.

Our portal for such time travel in Girton chapel is not the TARDIS, but, rather, the Advent ring. Over the course of an hour, I take the college on a journey through the Sundays of Advent, each with its distinct theme, its reading, music, and poetry, and I light the Advent candles one by one as we go, until, poised before the central candle, I bring us to the brink of what the physicists happily call 'the event-horizon'.

Then, amid a hushed and darkened chapel, shimmering with candles, we imagine ourselves at midnight mass, and hear the Mistress read St John's prologue, that mysterious prose-poem wherein the beginning and the end of all things is made richly available, both in and out of time, for all of us here in the middle.

'Can I get there by candlelight?' Perhaps candlelight is itself the best way to make this journey – not to Babylon, but back from the Babel of all our seasonal crush and pressure, back to Bethlehem, and the silent stars.

For there is always mystery and beauty in the lighting of a candle: the quickened little wick suddenly resplendent in light that must always be received from another. Coleridge, at his lowest ebb, bedridden after a long illness, in 1801, comparing himself to the 'Cold Snuff on the circular Rim of a Brass Candle-stick', could still recall how he, like the candle, 'was once cloathed and mitred with flame', and even the memory of that light began to rekindle him.

I feel the same way in this season, glad to light whatever candles I can rather than simply curse the darkness. So, though I won't breathe a word of it out of season, beyond the confines of the college, or contribute in any way to the crass commercialism of ever-earlier Christmases; though I will keep Advent as a blessed, low, subfusc season of expectation – keep it, as Betjeman rightly said, as '*waiting* Advent'; though there will be no decorations in our house till Christmas Eve; nevertheless, I will be glad to anticipate the Great Light a little in Girton

> … while the light fails
> On a winter's afternoon, in a secluded chapel …

30

The Full English

One of the pleasures of familiar texts, often repeated, known by heart without there ever having been a time when you consciously memorised them, is that they are richly available whenever you summon them, and they sometimes come unbidden to your mind in idle moments: while waiting for trains or buses, or on some short familiar walk.

So it was that I found the words of the General Thanksgiving praying themselves happily through me as I waited for an early-morning bus to Cambridge – a bus that, I hoped, would get me to college in time for breakfast. As this great prayer sounded through my mind, I was particularly struck by the words 'most humble and hearty thanks', and especially by the word *hearty*. It's a word with some gusto and relish in it, as in the phrase 'The condemned man ate a hearty breakfast.'

It set me thinking that, if thanksgivings were breakfasts, then the General Thanksgiving would not be some slender option with a little muesli and a couple of grapes; no, it would be 'The Full English'! It manages to get generous helpings of almost everything on to the plate; for it is the least stingy, the most inclusive of prayers. I love all its *alls*: '*all* mercies', '*all* thy goodness and loving-kindness to us and to *all* men', '*all* the blessings of this life', '*all* honour and glory'.

I relish the fact that it is a 'both/and' kind of prayer rather than the more parsimonious 'either/or' option. I savour all those lovely doublings, like double helpings in a generous

B&B: 'the means of grace *and* the hope of glory', '*not only* with our lips, *but in* our lives'. Why choose between 'the means of grace' and 'the hope of glory' when there's room for both on the plate? Yes, this prayer's main ingredient is a thanksgiving for eternal salvation, but it also contains generous side servings of creation, preservation, and all the blessings of this life, which is just what you need to work up an appetite and prepare the palate for 'the inestimable love' and the 'redemption' that are waiting for you when you've finished the blessings of this life.

The difference, of course, is that when it comes to breakfast you can, I regret to say, have too much of a good thing, but you can never have too much thanksgiving. A hearty breakfast might leave you a little weighted and ponderous, but a hearty thanksgiving tends to lighten your step, and give you edge and appetite for all that the day might bring.

If thanksgivings were breakfasts ... I was just pursuing this idea a little further, wondering whether the Scottish grace 'Some hae meat and cannae eat ...' might be a kind of porridge, and whether the '*Benedictus benedicat*', which is our college grace, might be something classic, but still lighter – say, Eggs Benedict – when I noticed that my bus had arrived, for which I gave most humble and hearty thanks.

31

Things Old and New

I was visiting Salisbury the other day, to give a talk at Sarum College – that gem of the cathedral close, with its elegant seventeenth-century frontage and its glorious bookshop – and afterwards I was taken out to supper.

My hosts obviously knew their man, as they took me to a local hostelry. How much better to be in a particular, peculiar, timeworn 'local' than in some ersatz, identikit chain whose corporate image and plastic décor could be anywhere and nowhere.

And this particular inn was very fine. I knew from the moment I had to dip under the lintel of its low door and saw the blackened and irregular beams criss-crossing the old brickwork, with here and there the remnants of dark linen-fold panelling, that this would be an inn to savour.

And so it proved, as the landlord drew me a pint of porter and we made our way into one of the snugs in its maze-like interior. While we waited for supper to be served, I drew up from my memory a verse from a ballade I had written some years ago, which celebrated just such a place as this, and all the skill, the story, and tradition that it preserves:

> I love the mullioned snug, the brewers dray
> And all the tapster's tacit craft and lore.
> To reach a village inn when skies are grey,
> To step out of the rain and through the door,

> To feel the warmth, to tread the stone-flagged floor,
> And sit beside the fire and take our ease,
> This is the bliss our little life is for,
> I'll have another pint of porter please.

This Salisbury inn turned out to be very old indeed – older than the cathedral itself; for it was one of the first four houses in 'New Sarum', built to lodge the masons when the present cathedral was begun in 1221. But the best thing about it was its name; for, being the oldest hostelry in the place, it was, of course, called the New Inn.

It's a good rule of thumb, in England at least, that anything prefaced 'Ye Olde' was probably knocked up in the last decade or so, but that anything still called 'new' is likely to be very old indeed. Witness New College, Oxford, founded in 1379, and so one of the oldest colleges; or, for that matter, the New Forest, proclaimed *Nova Foresta* in the Domesday book of 1086, though already ancient then, yet through all the centuries of its decays, its flourishings, and its renewals, still happily called 'new'.

But there was better still to come. For, back at Sarum College after supper, I took up in my hands another of these ancient things that we still call 'new': the oldest and the best of all of them. Older than the New Inn, it was already centuries old before the proclamation of the New Forest; older still than the oldest English cathedral, and yet, in its own way, as welcoming as that old hostelry; as living and mysterious as that old forest; as hallowed and numinous as the old cathedrals; and as new and renewing as all of them.

For that evening I held in my hands that ancient book that we still call the New Testament.

32

In a Country Churchyard

The other evening, I found myself straying through the lovely churchyard of St Mary's, Linton, with its path between rows of ancient yews, its further reaches bordered by light woods on one side and the clear flowing stream of the Granta on the other; and its many gravestones and memorials, most of them mottled, lichen-covered, their inscriptions and outlines not so much fading as greening, deepening, somehow merging with the soil in which they stand, the place in which they are planted.

I paused there, just to savour the twilight, the shimmer of shadow and light, the patter of leaves, and found both the place and the time had summoned unbidden the resonant lines of Thomas Gray's 'Elegy Written in a Country Churchyard':

> Now fades the glimm'ring landscape on the sight,
> And all the air a solemn stillness holds …

Certainly, there was a rich hush, and I could see in Linton, just as Gray had done in Stoke Poges:

> Beneath those rugged elms, that yew-tree's shade,
> Where heaves the turf in many a mould'ring heap,
> Each in his narrow cell for ever laid,
> The rude forefathers of the hamlet sleep.

But, of course, Gray, in that poem, goes on to challenge his own phrase about 'the rude forefathers of the hamlet', and to wonder what might have been achieved by so many who were denied education and opportunity in his unequal society. He thinks of some 'village-Hampden', or 'mute inglorious Milton', who never ruled or wrote because

> Chill Penury repress'd their noble rage,
> And froze the genial current of the soul.

As I stood there, I reflected that, even though more than 270 years have passed since Gray stood in the twilight of a country churchyard, and even though the education and literacy for which he was pleading are so much more widespread, it is still true that 'chill penury' holds back and denies opportunity to so many – perhaps more so now than when I first read and loved this poem 40 years ago.

As Gray's memorable and sonorous lines continued to unroll in my mind, my reflections took another turn. His poem is not only a eulogy for the excluded poor, but also, as one might expect, a moving *memento mori*, an unflinching and chastened attention to mortality of the kind that is almost forbidden now:

> The boast of heraldry, the pomp of pow'r,
> And all that beauty, all that wealth e'er gave,
> Awaits alike th' inevitable hour.
> The paths of glory lead but to the grave.

Yet as these lines sounded through my mind, and I gazed around, in the last of the light, at the many graves all mossed and green in this lovely place, I had a sense not of morbidity, or of melancholy, but of richness, of fullness. The contemplation of finitude only deepened my sense of plenitude, of the sheer and undeserved abundance of my being here: a sense that all of it must be savoured: this churchyard in 'the viridian darkness of its yews', the little stream I would cross as I left, and, beyond it, an opening door and the welcoming light of home.

33

The Return of the Native

I am writing this from a hotel room high above the streets of
Calgary, that strange splinter of Texas embedded in the heart
of Canada. This is not the season for the Calgary Stampede,
but there are still rangey figures in Stetsons and cowboy boots
striding through the freezing wind that channels down the
canyons of those high-rise towers thrown skywards by oil
money.

Happily, the horizon also holds the awe-inspiring profile of
the distant Rocky Mountains, whose eternally snowy peaks
were there before every human endeavour, and will be there
when our towers have tumbled.

Meanwhile, though, I'm enjoying the Western flavour of this
northern city. I'm in Canada for a tour, 'Songs and Sonnets', in
which the Canadian singer-songwriter Steve Bell and I take turns
at singing and reciting – though, happily for me, he has set a
number of my poems to music, and so my recitation is followed
by something more tuneful.

This tour also carries for me a personal pull and flow; for it
started in Hamilton Ontario, exactly 50 years after my family
arrived there in 1967, when I was ten. It was there that I spent
my early teens. In the past few days, I have recovered many
vivid memories of my childhood and youth: my first winter,
which I thought would never end (I had been brought up in
Africa); the purchase of my first LP, a Bob Dylan classic, which
I never wanted to end; my first guitar: a cheap plywood affair;

and, stumbling along with its three chords, my first attempts at poetry.

Leaving Canada had somehow sealed or frozen all these memories. Now, on the return of the native, they have been released.

I found again a trail I used to hike into a steep ravine and across a narrow bridge over a little creek. It was all still there, a little smaller, but also sharply focused, utterly familiar, and poignant. I stood on the bridge and watched the creek flow by beneath me as I had done all those years ago. I knew somehow that all one's life one is standing on another bridge, above the stream of time.

For, as Geoffrey Hill says in one of his beautiful *Tenebrae* sonnets, we 'stay amidst the things that will not stay'. Everything flows through us and from us. Each moment comes towards us, freighted with its unique burden of beauty and sorrow, yet somehow still afloat, carried perilously along the stream of time; it comes mysteriously, and mysteriously it goes, slipping away beneath and behind us almost before we've seen it.

And yet we remain. Here we still are on the strange bridge of our selfhood, our mysterious I-am-ness, watching the river flow.

As I – a grey-haired man whom my ten-year-old self would not have recognised – stood there on that little bridge in Hamilton, I knew that I could still recognise him, and that, indeed, he was still with me on the bridge. I knew that, when I climbed back up the ravine and back on the road for this tour, something of that ten-year-old's quick eye, his bright energy, and his immense longing would be alive in me again.

34

My Books

'Tis dark: quick pattereth the flaw-blown sleet.'

Keats's scene-setting for *The Eve of St Agnes* – a January poem if ever there was one – could serve just as well to set the scene where I sit snug in my study, surrounded and comforted by my books, while fitful gusts fling the weather against my window.

But I have warmth, lamplight, the sleeping dogs at my feet, and, best of all, my books as familiar friends; volumes of every shape and size, some elegantly bound, some worn and splitting, each with a story to tell, not only within their pages, but about their pages, too.

They carry the memories of when and where I bought them, the different times I read them, the friends with whom I read them. They are none of them catalogued or constrained into rank and file by any system. I let them stand on shelves or lie open on tables and chairs in any order, as happy chance or my own fancy finds them. Sometimes, I feel sure, they consort together and shift around when I'm not in the room. I'm certain I left John Donne safe in George Herbert's improving company, but here he is on the table consorting with T. S. Eliot, again!

This evening, my pleasure in books themselves was intensified, when, idly turning the pages of Leigh Hunt, I came upon his little essay 'My Books', and read the opening sentence:

> Sitting, last winter, among my books, and walled round with all the comfort and protection which they and my fireside could afford me…I began to consider how I loved the authors of those books; how I loved them, too, not only for the imaginative pleasures they afforded me, but for their making me love the very books themselves.

The very same scene. I felt as though he were here with me, or I there with him.

In that amiable essay, Hunt also remembers the friends with whom he shared his reading and his library. He tells how Charles Lamb loved his old folio of Chapman's *Homer* so much that he gave it a kiss (as well he might – for it was this same volume that gave Hunt's other friend Keats such delight that he wrote the immortal sonnet 'On First Looking into Chapman's Homer').

'Much have I travelled in the realms of gold,' I could say with Keats, but my realms of gold include Keats himself, Hunt, and their mutual friend Shelley; for what makes Hunt's little essay so poignant is that it was written in Italy just after Shelley's death. Hunt, who had stood on the shore with Byron as Shelley's body was burned, tells us that it was a volume of Keats which he himself had lent to Shelley that they found in his pocket when he was recovered from the sea. Shelley had promised that it would always be with him till Hunt saw him again.

Hunt says one more thing, to close the essay. He had once asked Shelley what book he would most like to save, and the famous atheist replied, 'The oldest book, the Bible.' 'It was a monument to him', Hunt says, 'of the earliest, most lasting, and most awful aspirations of humanity.'

So I laid down my Leigh Hunt, moved by that great radical
to pick up and open, once more, the oldest book.

35

On Poetry and Cheese

I enjoyed Richard Harries's review of the latest volume of T. S. Eliot's letters in *The Church Times* and I particularly savoured a sentence from near the end of that review: 'He wrote a strong letter to *The Times* in support of Stilton, and remarked that one of the purposes of life was in discovering new cheeses.'

One feels that there is something still right with the world when someone can write a strong letter to *The Times* in support of a particular cheese, and, of course, one could hardly write a *mild* letter in defence of so strong a cheese.

But Eliot's stern defence of Stilton put me in mind of G. K. Chesterton's wonderful essay about finding himself in an inn in the village of Stilton, only to be told that they had no Stilton available. He makes that a parable for our times. It is, as he says, 'a strange allegory of England as she is now; this little town that had lost its glory; and forgotten, so to speak, the meaning of its own name'. And, then, channelling his inner Wordsworth, Chesterton breaks into a sonnet beginning 'Stilton, thou shouldst be living at this hour … England has need of thee.'

It was also in that essay, I think, that Chesterton made his famous remark 'The Poets have been mysteriously silent about cheese.' This is very true, and it's a pity that Eliot's love of cheese didn't find expression in his poetry, though perhaps the phrase 'or even a very good dinner', from 'The Dry Salvages', implies, in Eliot's cryptic way, some excellent cheese.

Musing on Chesterton's remark about the silence of the poets, I began to wonder about the poetic qualities and attractions of cheese itself, and, like Chesterton before me, I found that my musings had taken the form of a sonnet:

The poets have been silent about cheese
Because, whilst every subject is the message,
Cheese is the very medium of their work.
We drink in language with our mother's milk,
But poets curdle words until they bite,
With substance and a flavour of their own:
So Donne is sharp and Geoffrey Hill is sour,
Larkin acerbic, Tennyson has power
(But only late at night, taken with port).
I like them all, and sample every sort
From creamy Keats with his 'mossed cottage trees',
Tasting the words themselves like cottage cheese,
To Eliot, difficult, in cold collations,
Crumbling, and stuffed with other folk's quotations.

I'm sure that readers of this book will disagree with me about my attribution of particular cheeses to particular poets, but, then, what better way to spend an evening than to gather a good variety of cheeses, a fine selection of poetry, and a few of those excellent wines that bring out the best in both, and enjoy a few hours in good company testing their qualities and pairing them more appropriately?

It would be a pleasant pastime for what Eliot called, again in 'The Dry Salvages', 'the evening circle in the winter gaslight'.

36

Homing

I am coming to the end of my Canadian jaunt, and yearning to be 'back in Blighty'. I have written in my *Church Times* column about reviving memories of my earlier Canadian life, about the energising thrill of reconnecting with an inner child, standing on the bridge where I stood 50 years ago, about how I rekindled something of that child's quick eye, and deep longing.

But, as Wordsworth says, 'the Child is the father of the Man', and the man wants to go home. So tomorrow's homeward flight can't come a moment too soon.

I know that the airports, like the railway stations and the motorways, will be full of Christmas travellers, as this season releases in all of us a deep homing instinct. But, even as my mind starts playing Paul Simon's 'Homeward Bound' on its inner soundtrack, I hear another voice in the mix, pointing away from all the sentiment and nostalgia, pointing instead to a strange Christmas paradox.

It is the voice of G. K. Chesterton, and he is reciting his little poem 'The House of Christmas':

> For men are homesick in their homes,
> And strangers under the sun,
> And they lay their heads in a foreign land
> Whenever the day is done.

But that disturbing paradox about our homelessness in this world, our exiled longing for heaven, is followed by another stranger, but more comforting, paradox: the Christmas mystery, through which heaven has come home to us:

> A Child in a foul stable,
> Where the beasts feed and foam;
> Only where He was homeless
> Are you and I at home.

The hotel lobby where I am writing this is saturated with the saccharine kitsch of Christmas music on repeat; I never want to hear another sampled sleigh bell or the rhyme of 'Jolly' and 'Holly'.

And yet, with Chesterton on my mind, the voice of Chris Rea, which has just emerged from the muzak, singing 'Driving Home for Christmas', begins to make strange sense. Chesterton, and perhaps Rea himself, would enjoy the irony of this song playing in the lounge of a swish hotel, for Rea wrote it 29 years ago in the passenger seat of a clapped-out mini, stuck in motorway traffic, trying to get to Middlesbrough. He didn't even think he had a song, let alone a Christmas hit, and it wasn't released for another ten years.

But now I hear him in a Winnipeg hotel, his gruff voice strangely harmonising with GKC, because all three of us know that the journey home doesn't stop when the Christmas journey is over and we reach our home address. We know, with T. S. Eliot, that 'home is where one starts from'. Yet we have hope for the longer journey, and the true Homecoming.

So, as Chris Rea fades out in the lobby, I turn up the volume on my inner soundtrack and hear again the great hope disclosed in the last verse of Chesterton's Christmas song:

> To an open house in the evening
> Home shall men come,
> To an older place than Eden
> And a taller town than Rome.
> To the end of the way of the wandering star,
> To the things that cannot be and that are,
> To the place where God was homeless
> And all men are at home.

37

God Speed the Plough

One Sunday, I was called on, in my capacity as poet, to assist at the blessing of a plough on an old hill-farm in Essex. I had driven through winding and increasingly narrow and shadowed lanes, past quickset hedgerows, and up the steep farm track, admiring the rambling old farmhouse, which seemed pieced together from every period in the past 400 years, and yet still at home with itself.

But this was no quaint exercise in picturesque nostalgia, blessing the rusted wings and single blade of some hand-guided horse-drawn plough that hadn't seen service in years (though there was just such a plough in the barn). The plough we were blessing meant business: it was a great long apparatus of paired bright sharp circular blades, capable of churning through the earth as efficiently as the old 'screw steamers' churned the ocean, and yoked behind an enormous modern tractor.

Yes, there had been a sense of tradition and continuity in the service; I had read Seamus Heaney's poem 'Follower', with its lovely opening:

> My father worked with a horse-plough,
> His shoulders globed like a full sail strung
> Between the shafts and the furrow.

The farmer had a display, in one of his barns, of relics and artefacts from the continuous human flourishing on his acres since Roman times. But, for now, we all stood in the muddy farmyard in our wellies, ready to bless today's hi-tech farm machinery, the present labour, the contemporary human flourishing.

And, just before she came to bless the plough, the priest asked everyone gathered there to bring forward, and hold beside it, the implements of their own work. Gardeners came with trowels; a man who had been coppicing the woods and laying hedges that morning came forward with a bright-bladed axe and the other fascinating tools of his trade; children held out model tractors; and, taken by surprise, I held out my pen.

'Let us each offer to God in our hearts our own work,' she said.

'God speed the plough!' and 'God speed the plough!' was our response.

Afterwards, I read them my sonnet 'Daily Bread', which remembers

> … the ones who plough and sow,
> Who pick and plant and package whilst we sleep,
> With slow back-breaking labour, row by row,
> And send away to others all they reap,
> We know that these unseen who meet our needs
> Are all themselves the fingers of your hand …
> What if we glimpsed you daily in their toil
> And found and thanked and served you through them all?

I don't know what the theologians and the philosophers

would say had happened there, how they would discern the difference that a blessing makes, but I do know that, somehow, that farmer would turn the soil of God's good ground with a renewed sense of blessing, and the gardeners return to their gardens with a new awareness, for I felt it, too.

When I had come home, washed the mud from my boots, and was sitting at my desk, that plough-blessed pen poised in hand, I had some sense of a difference made – some sense that, with this pen, like Heaney before me, I might dig a little deeper.

38

A Bench in Aldeburgh

Just above the steep flight of the 'town steps' in Aldeburgh, there is a little bench, set to one side, sheltered over and nestled into the green bank of the hill. There you can sit, snug from the wind, resting from the effort of climbing the steps, and gaze across the little town's glorious roofscape, and out past the timbered Moot House and those dark huts where the daily catch is smoked and sold, out to the sea itself.

The roofs are a pleasing assortment of shapes and sizes: little cottages, substantial town houses, and odd buildings built into corners and gaps, almost all tiled in old, red clay tiles which have weathered and variegated into as many fine gradations of red, mottled yellow, brown, and ochre as one might find in the soil itself.

In all their different shapes and sizes, angles and pitches, the roofs slope down to the main street and the seafront itself, where peculiar little watchtowers and turrets with miniature castellations add to the variety. Sitting there, one can imagine, for a moment, all the other varieties of homeliness and human life packed under those roofs; the people coming and going, departing, journeying, and homing again.

And beyond it all, just audible, the surging of the sea on its shingly shore, at once restless and soothing, as it was to Keats when, dying in Rome, he seemed to see

> The moving waters at their priestlike task
> Of pure ablution round earth's human shores

We only go to Aldeburgh once a year, to stay for a few days in January, another exhausted clergy couple in post-Christmas recovery mode. But I always take the time to sit on that bench, absorb the view, and smoke a meditative pipe.

And I have found that, over the years, by fondness and familiarity, that little nook and its entrancing view have become available to me wherever I am. Trudging some bleak street, drained and laden, or ensconced on the upper deck of a crowded bus, I have a door that opens, unbeknown to my fellow passengers, to a secret otherwhere; I have only to pass through it to find that I am present there; for the place is present in me.

Who can trace that mysterious transposition whereby an outer place becomes an inner one? A spiritual alchemy, a sublimation and transference has happened gradually, yet suddenly the growing soul has found herself another nesting place. So Yeats found, treading 'the pavements grey' in London while his whole inner being heard lake water lapping on the isle of Innisfree; and Joyce, blinding in Zurich, could walk down Grafton Street and number all the Dublin doors.

'When you pray', Jesus says, 'go into your room and shut the door, and pray in secret, and your Father, who is in secret, will reward you.' And one part, at least, of that secret, certainly part of that reward, is that the inside of the inner door is bigger than the outside, as was the door once, to a stable.

39

A Winter Ale Festival

I have been enjoying the Cambridge Winter Ale Festival, not only for the ales but also for the whole atmosphere. To step through the door out of a dreich January drizzle into the warm fug, the gregarious clatter and chatter of enthusiasts at play, is a pleasure.

This festival is on a smaller scale than the tented summer fest, and all the better for it; but there's still more than enough variety both in ales and ale drinkers. Indeed, a private pleasure of mine comes in matching the quirky names and vivid descriptions in the list of beers with the appearance and likely personalities of my fellow enthusiasts.

There is a man in the corner with a weathered face, a mass of grey hair, and a mischievous twinkle in his eyes who seems a good match for 'Old Nogg: warming, mild-bodied, with a slightly nutty flavour'. Although contrary to the clichéd image, it's not all bearded men in woolly jumpers, and the young of both sexes are well represented.

I notice that the beer list has an American-hopped IPA which is described as 'Hazy, golden, with a big head' – well, I can think of a couple of candidates for that, here and in the United States – and there are a fair few at this fest who would match up to Crafty Beer's wonderfully named Sauvignon Blonde. It's as well I'm not allowed to smoke my pipe in here, otherwise someone might already have me down as 'Smokin' Angel: complex, malty, dark, with smoky aroma'.

This festival, and hundreds like it, are testimony to CAMRA, the Campaign for Real Ale: a grassroots revolution, and one of the earliest and most effective consumer pressure groups; a vast network of ordinary people who wouldn't put up with the standardised, ersatz, advertised beers foisted on them by the big breweries, but preferred the local, the traditional, the particular, and sometimes peculiar character of a living beer, not a gassed-up pasteurised counterfeit.

Pulling on my pint of Marcus Aurelius (you know you're in Cambridge when there's a beer called Marcus Aurelius), I found myself remembering the opening lines of Blake's *Little Vagabond*:

> Dear Mother, dear Mother, the Church is cold,
> But the Ale-house is healthy & pleasant & warm;
> Besides I can tell where I am use'd well ...

And I wondered if the Church might take a leaf out of CAM-RA's book. Not for the first time, I began to fantasise about founding CAMRE, the Campaign for Real Evangelism. Eschewing identikit evangelistic courses and formulae, or fizzy American imports, CAMRE would revive living local traditions, each as distinct as a local ale but each carrying the active ferment of the gospel; stirring and refreshing good news.

After all, Golden Grain, Living Water, and Secretly Working Yeast, the three essentials in every distinct brew, are also all essential images and parables of the Kingdom. Perhaps we should see each small parish as a kind of microbrewery, combining an ancient recipe with local ingredients for a lively, distinct, and refreshing gift to its own community.

And maybe CAMRE could be as welcoming as CAMRA to the thirsty newcomer who has so much to learn and to savour. I'll be first up for the festival.

40

A Hidden Valley

A while ago, I drove north to Wydale Hall, a lovely remote retreat house nestled into the head of a valley on the edge of the
North York Moors. It was, unfortunately, on a day when winter chose to infringe on the rights of spring and fling its last
worst flurries of snow at us, like someone who has stormed
out of a room and then storms back in again because they've
thought of one more really cutting thing to say.

So I drove into an almost complete white-out of intermittent
blizzards on roads that had lost all their markings, at first
in crawling traffic on the main roads, and then on roads so
lonely, and as white as the fields around them, that I feared
I might have lost the road altogether and would end up in
some frozen ditch or hedgerow. But, at length, I found, and
somehow surmounted, the steep track that led me up, far later
than I had planned, to the welcoming lights of the old hall,
and was ushered in to warmth, comfort, and rest by the kindly
warden.

Of course, I'd missed all the scenery through which I'd been
driving, because I was snow-blinded and just gripping the
steering wheel in grim determination, trying to hold the road;
but the next morning I saw the little valley from my window,
pristine and sparkling in the fresh snow, stretching away to
distant hills, breathtakingly beautiful. And, the day after that,
restored by strong spring sunshine, the same vista was new
again, clothed and folded in fresh green, sudden, unexpected,

and, as Philip Larkin says, 'Utterly unlike the snow.'

That second day, I took the little path from the house and along the valley edge and then up over its lip, and had scarcely gone five steps when, as I looked back, the valley seemed to have disappeared, together with its graceful house, so completely tucked away as it was, in the steep folds of the hill.

It reminded me of the description in *The Hobbit* of how they come upon the hidden valley of Rivendell, searching apparently in vain among the stony paths until they come to the lip of the vale, the path drops steeply, the air warms, and they hear the welcome sound of running water and glimpse, as dusk falls, the lights shining in 'the last homely house'. The similarities didn't end there, and, by the end of my three days at Wydale, I knew that Tolkien's lovely account of Elrond's Rivendell was true of this place, too: 'His house was perfect, whether you liked food, or sleep, or work, or storytelling, or singing, or just thinking best, or a pleasant mixture of them all. Evil things did not come into that valley.'

On that retreat, we did indeed have a pleasant mixture of all those things. It set me thinking that perhaps all retreats, whether or not the retreat house is physically in a hidden valley like this one, are a kind of sojourn in Rivendell.

We take shelter in the folds of a sacred place, and, although it seems soon to disappear from sight as we take our onward journey, its hidden goodness is still concealed in the folds and contours of our souls, and, from time to time, we can drop back down, out of the weather and weariness of the world, and hear the stream running, and find warmth and welcome in a house that, in some sense, we have never left.

41

A Serendipitous Island

Earlier, I wrote about stepping out of a chill January drizzle into the snug and fuggy atmosphere of a winter ale festival. Now I write from a rickety wooden terrace in bright sunshine, the tropical heat gratefully tempered by a gentle breeze wafting in from the Indian Ocean, whose lovely green waves lapse and spill on bright white sands just below me, and the same breeze carries the delightful scents of frangipani and hibiscus, and mingled voices, calling variously in Singhalese, Tamil, and English, as merchants ply their wares, and a snake-charmer gathers a little crowd beneath a coconut tree on the astonishing island of Sri Lanka.

The man responsible for this remarkable transition is S. T. Coleridge. It so happened that, on the memorable occasion when I just missed my albatross in Wells, my talk there on Coleridge was heard by someone from the Fairway Galle Literary Festival, and, on the strength of that talk, he sent an invitation that would lift me off my own island and bring me to his: from Somerset to Sri Lanka in one fell swoop.

That little serendipity seems fitting for an island once known by the Persian name of Serendib, from which our own 'serendipity' is derived.

How Coleridge would have loved this island! It has its own beautiful lighthouse, green hill, and fine white temples and churches, which echo 'the kirk, the hill, and the light-house top' in his poem. But perhaps his most delightful surprise would have been to discover how many of the islanders here know and love *Rime of the Ancient Mariner*. Happily, my talk on Coleridge was, in every sense, warmly received, but it was the Indian and Sri Lankan audience, even more than the Westerners, who leaned forward and could be seen chanting along with the passages of the poem which I cited, its phrases as deeply embedded in their own minds as in mine. After the talk, they crowded round to tell me how I had revived their childhood memories; for they had all loved and learned the poem at school.

Coleridge would also certainly have enjoyed the hospitality. When I gave a poetry reading, the festival arranged for a chef to cook different cakes and sweetmeats to go with different tea-blends – not only from the famous plantations here, but from around the world.

Coleridge imagined his mariner as completing a circumnavigation, and, in the latter part of the story, his hero would have been sailing through the Indian Ocean, perhaps in sight of this island, propelled by the deep Spirit beneath the keel and accompanied by two aery Daemons who fly above him and look down from the air at the little vessel speeding through the sea.

Coleridge had to imagine what that ocean would look like from above, but by another serendipity I saw it for myself; for, on the third day, I was taken up in a small aeroplane, out beyond the island, to where the sea changes from green to blue, colours as clear and sparkling as the emeralds and sapphires displayed by the island's many jewellers, and there I saw from the air the little ships, and, disporting themselves in the deep, two magnificent blue whales.

But the last and best serendipity came when I celebrated a bilingual Candlemas at All Saints', Galle, and heard for myself, in Singhalese, old Simeon's proclamation that Christ would be a light to the nations – both theirs and mine.

42

Finding the Source

There is a fascination in following rivers upstream towards their source, whether it's an epic exploration of *terra incognita* or a country walk over familiar ground. To be accompanied by a stream, to have a sense of following it towards its hidden origin, has a draw that is about more than outer topography: it taps into our yearning towards the mystery from which all things flow.

And the flow of the stream itself becomes, by gradual association, an expression, an outer image, of that other stream, the stream of our consciousness as we walk; both streams have their pools and eddies, their little rushes forward, their passages where all is clouded or covered, alternating with stretches of complete clarity.

I felt this kinship between the outer and the inner very strongly while reading Katharine Norbury's moving book *The Fish Ladder*, a work that plays into that fascination with finding the source, in a close and gripping account of a series of journeys upstream towards the sources of various rivers, undertaken by a mother and daughter together. The writing is very vivid: 'I heard a sibilant trickle, a mischievous chatter as the stream spattered over gravel, and the white cloud once again pressed around us. The only colour was in the bright moss, visible once more at our feet.'

These lines made me feel as though I were there, invisibly, as the mother and daughter make their way alongside a stream that keeps disappearing and reappearing, towards its numinous and beautiful source: a holy well.

The pleasure of reading in itself is also a kind of drawing towards a source. As one immerses oneself in the flow of the prose, one wonders what it would be like to travel upstream of the writing and encounter the writer.

As it happens, I had just that experience – not on the banks of an English river, but on the shore of the Indian Ocean; for Katharine and I were both speakers at the Galle Literary Festival in Sri Lanka, and had been asked to do a joint session on literature and landscape.

We are living in a golden age of nature writing, and Katharine, one of its representatives, was there to talk about this present flowering in writers such as Robert Macfarlane and Helen Macdonald. My task was to take us a little further upstream, to the works of Wordsworth and Coleridge, and to show how their reimagining of the links between outer and inner worlds had opened a channel for the work that is going on now.

Meeting Katharine and the other writers at the festival made me realise that my own quest to 'find the source' was not ultimately about meeting the authors themselves, or even exploring their literary sources, but, rather, about discovering that none of us, as writers, is ever the source or well-head of our own work. Instead, we gather as fellow pilgrims on the banks of a river whose source we can never trace; for it is always just upstream of utterance.

The quest in *The Fish Ladder* was inspired by Neil M. Gunn's book *The Well at the World's End* (a title that Gunn had borrowed from William Morris). But, for a writer, the world's end, and its beginning, is in the moment when we take up the pen, and our own deepest sources are hidden from us. We come to them afresh each time we take out a notebook, its blank pages open and empty, like two hands cupped at a well.

43

A Doorkeeper

I returned recently to my old church of St Edward, King and Martyr, in Cambridge to take the funeral of a faithful and much loved member of the congregation. As a sidesman, Donald Lynden-Bell had always been a genial, kindly, welcoming presence, ushering people in, handing them their order of service – setting himself aside and gesturing inwards towards the beautiful, numinous space of the church.

He was also, as it happens, one of the greatest minds of our time: an astronomer and mathematician who had established the link between black holes and quasars, and shown their role in the formation of galaxies.

As the church began to fill, not only with his family and friends, with the many distinguished scientists who had been his students, and as the tributes began, it became clear that he had also been a kind of doorkeeper in his work as a scientist and teacher: ushering people in, explaining what they needed to know – but ultimately setting himself aside and gesturing upwards towards the beautiful, numinous space of the firmament of heaven.

He had been one of the subjects of the wonderful documentary film *Starmen: Bringing the Universe Down to Earth*. Alison Rose, the filmmaker, had flown over from Canada so that she could be at the funeral and read the lesson from Ecclesiasticus, from Lynden-Bell's own well-worn copy of the Apocrypha: 'The beauty of heaven, the glory of the stars, an ornament giving light in the highest places of the Lord.'

Lynden-Bell had been so absorbed in his attention to, and wonder at, the cosmos, and at the beauty of the mathematics that he discerned underpinning it, so glad to share that knowledge and enthusiasm, directing the eye and attention of his hearers away from himself and towards the immense mystery on whose surface we live, that he seemed scarcely aware that he himself was a wonder – that he, too, was 'an ornament giving light in the highest places'.

He was the same man in his faith as he was in his science: open, attentive, keen to ask questions and explore, not willing to press propositions further than he thought they could go, but never losing his sense of wonder. In my address, I read a passage from Coleridge, another inveterate stargazer, which seemed to link Donald's worlds together. At the end of his *Biographia Literaria*, his own personal testament, Coleridge affirmed:

> that Religion passes out of the ken of Reason only where the eye of Reason has reached its own Horizon; and that Faith is then but its continuation: even as the Day softens away into the sweet Twilight, and Twilight, hushed and breathless, steals into the Darkness. It is Night, sacred Night! The upraised Eye views only the starry Heaven which manifests itself alone: and the outward Beholding is fixed on the sparks twinkling in the aweful depth, though Suns of other Worlds, only to preserve the Soul steady and collected in its pure *Act* of inward Adoration to the great I AM.

And so a doorkeeper in the house of the Lord, a doorkeeper in the house of Science, passed at last through the door of the cosmos and was welcomed into his Father's house.

44

Learning Their Letters

I still like to write some things by hand, though my handwriting is not very good.

There is something in the forming of the letters themselves, in the contrast of ink and paper, and maybe some muscle-memory that engages a connection with one's own deep past, with the child first learning to form these letters, and perhaps with the deeper past of our culture, with the whole long beautiful history of literacy.

I was moved to discover that, at the height of his fame, Charles Dickens could still consciously remember being taught by his mother to write. He said to his friend, and future biographer, John Forster: 'I faintly remember her teaching me the alphabet; and when I look upon the fat black letters in the primer, the puzzling novelty of their shapes, the easy good nature of 'O' and 'S' always seem to present themselves before me as they used to do.'

It's wonderful to be given this glimpse of the moment Dickens becomes, in every sense, a writer. Before the trauma of the blacking factory, before the parliamentary reporting, before the first sketches by Boz, here he is, a little child carefully forming the letters O and S, and already, in imagination, endowing these characters with character, with the 'easy good nature' that would be made immortal in Mr Pickwick.

And for Dickens, the sheer continuity of writing would have been clearer, since he continued throughout life to write all his novels on paper with a dip pen – as did C. S. Lewis, long after fountain pens were invented; for Lewis maintained that the pause to lift the pen and to dip it in ink every few lines gave him just the time he needed to revolve his thoughts and continue.

Hilaire Belloc, by contrast, celebrated his fountain pen as 'a pen that runs straight away like a willing horse, or a jolly little ship'. But all these writers were doing something in continuity with their childhood, whereas we, who press virtual keys on flat screens, have broken that line.

Dickens was not alone in feeling that the letters themselves had character, that there was something alive and magical about them. Rimbaud's famous sonnet about vowels has a similar sense, about the letters themselves; a vivid synesthesia, giving each vowel a different colour:

> *A noir, E blanc, I rouge, U vert, O bleu: voyelles.*

It is interesting that his O is blue, like the beautiful O of the earth, glimpsed from the moon 85 years later.

In his poem 'Alphabets', Seamus Heaney, too, records vivid memories of learning his letters, though characteristically he looks from the letter to the world itself, and to the whole world as a kind of divine letter:

> Smells of inkwells rise in the classroom hush
> A globe in the window tilts like a coloured 'O'

For Christian writers, there is a still deeper meaning in the mystery of letters, the spell of spelling: that mystery whereby the world herself and all the letters, the lovely shapes and sounds that she contains, arise out of the Word. As George Herbert put it: 'Thy Word is all, if we could spell.'

45

Our Time to Turn

Even with an early Lent like this, one senses with relief the turning of the year. On that Valentine's Ash Wednesday, it was the snowdrops and aconites rising bravely out of the cold ground, rather than the hothouse roses wilting on garage forecourts, that lifted my heart.

And now, at last, the earth is breathing other flowers into being, the crocuses are bright beneath the trees in college, and everywhere I sense that warming and stirring, that rustling in the hedgerows and scattering of birdsong through the gardens, as the last of winter lets go its grasp.

Lancelot Andrewes sensed just such a turning of the year, and of the heart, when Lent came in with the spring in 1619. In a beautiful Ash Wednesday sermon, a meditation on turning and returning, which strongly influenced Eliot's poem *Ash Wednesday*, Andrewes said:

> So 'it hath seemed good to the Holy Ghost' and to her to order there shall be a solemn set return once in the year at least. And reason; for once a year all things turn. And that once is now at this time, for now at this time is the turning of the year. In Heaven, the sun in his equinoctial line, the zodiac and all the constellations in it, do now turn about to the first point. The earth and all her plants, after a dead winter, return to the first and best season of the year. The creatures, the fowls of the air, the swallow and the turtle, and the crane and the stork, 'know their

seasons,' and make their just return at this time every year. Everything now turning, that we also would make it our time to turn to God in.

Andrewes's text was taken from Joel ('Turn you unto me with all your heart'), and there is indeed a kind of intimate and heartfelt yearning in his portrayal of God's longing for our return to him.

The words of this sermon were turning and returning in my mind when I was asked by the Canadian singer Steve Bell to write some lyrics for a song on his album *Pilgrimage*, a collection that he intended as a journey 'from Lent to Love'.

As we wrote the song together, I relished the thought that this was not only a transatlantic collaboration, but, with Andrewes in the mix, it crossed the centuries, too. And now, as the year turns again, the last verses of that song come back to me as I walk the lanes of our parish, contemplating the turn that Lent takes now towards the Passion:

> The time of year has come when all things turn.
> The sun returns to warm the wintry earth.
> The land revives, the plants and seedlings yearn
> Towards their rich beginnings and their birth.
>
> And will she turn, oh will she turn again?
> I hold my arms out wide upon the tree.
> And will she see me yearn to her through pain,
> And turn again and turn again to me?
>
> The grapes are swelling on the fruitful vine.
> The figs are ripe and low upon the bough.

I break the bread for her and pour the wine,
And all I Am is turned towards her now.

46

The Pocket Park

Just on the edge of Linton there is a wonderful patch of wilderness: a few acres of unsullied meadow and woodland, happily named the Pocket Park.

The clear stream of the Granta winds through it, with a little open meadow on one bank and a few copses of trees, small bosky dells, on the other. And, because it has never been fed with fertilisers or poisoned with pesticides, it is a haven for wild flowers, for rare and endangered flora and fauna.

As you wander there, you may glimpse a solitary grey heron, still as a hermit, or pause to hear the chaffinches chattering in the brakes and always you hear, just under all other sounds, somehow surfacing even through the rush of traffic on roads nearby, the music and murmur of the stream. It's the kind of place where you find yourself, almost unconsciously, reciting your psalms; for the green pastures, the trees planted by the waters, that fill the Psalter all seem to be bodied forth around you.

Small as it is, the Pocket Park feels somehow new and more capacious with each visit, renewed in the changing seasons. Resplendent and white in the early-March snow, it was a magical Narnian vista lacking only a lamp-post. Now, in this spring thaw, the Granta reasserts herself, and new pools spread abroad to reflect pale April skies. When young-leafed June arrives, these green groves will invite some happy re-enactment of *A Midsummer Night's Dream* on a balmy moonlit night.

It all makes me wish that there actually was such a thing as a Pocket Park: a park that one could keep folded away in one's pocket like a green handkerchief, and then take out and unfold on some grey pavement, where it would miraculously expand into an acre or two of refreshing greenery, rather like the briefcase carried by the wizard Newt Scamander in *Fantastic Beasts and Where to Find Them*. His innocent-looking leather holdall turns out to contain a whole world of wildlife, of which he is the steward and guardian. What fun it would be to take out my Pocket Park, unobtrusively unfold it, and, whispering some words of invocation, open its gate and bid the astonished passers-by to enter in!

Sadly, I cannot carry a park in my pocket, but, happily, I can carry a Psalter, and by whispering its opening formula of blessing and invocation, *Beatus vir*, I can, in my own small way, re-enter the *hortus conclusus*, the garden enclosed. Even on the flat plains of East Anglia, I can look up and see that 'the crags are a cover for the conies', and that 'he sendeth the springs into the rivers which run amongst the hills,' that 'the fowls of the air have their habitation and sing amongst the branches,' that 'he bringeth forth grass for the cattle and herb for the use of men.'

So, I've no need to envy Newt Scamander's magic satchel; for, even now, as I close my Psalter, I hear a visionary more powerful than any in the Wizarding World: Thomas Traherne, reminding me that I, too, have been given 'a cabinet of infinite value, equal in beauty, lustre and perfection to all its treasures … that centre of eternity, the Tree of Life.'

47

Some Time in York

After an absence of nearly two decades, I found myself back
in York, ensconced on an old bench, in the shelter of a para-
pet on the great medieval walls, smoking a meditative pipe,
admiring the way a shaft of evening sunlight broke through
grey clouds to illuminate the warm stone of the minster, and
reflecting a little on the nature of time.

York is a place where you can't help reflecting on time:
its strange eddies, and its long perspectives; for the place is
redolent of the past and yet keeps a living continuity with its
foundation.

Musing there, it seemed to me that time itself was less like
an arrow flying swiftly past, and more like a gradual accretion
of rich layers: layers of being; layers of action and passion,
thought and feeling, piling up gradually over the same place,
each layer leaving its trace, its record and pattern, like the
layers in sedimentary rock, or the rings on a great tree. I felt
that, far from flying or receding, time was simply deepening:
patiently, quietly, accumulating; that somehow all of it is
always still there, still available.

My day had begun with a visit to the Jorvik Museum, which
is vastly improved since my last visit; for now it includes a
carved stone cross, whose combined Christian motifs and
evocative animal figures witness in stone to the astonishing
tale of how those early Anglo-Saxon Christians found courage
to share their faith with the Norsemen who had been their

enemies, and how that faith clarified and redeemed the haunting stories in the Norse sagas – stories of a God who hung on the world tree, a sacrifice to himself.

The real drama of that museum, though, is the way it takes you down through the diggings, down through the layers of time. You start out standing on a glass floor above the Coppergate, where archaeologists, digging down past the discarded clay pipes of the eighteenth-century, past Jacobean tankards and the old Tudor timbers, down past the debris of the high middle ages, had uncovered, at last, the bare bones, the clean lines, sharp axes, and rune-written sword-blades of Viking York. Then, they take you down in carriages that are something like your own personal Tardis, to see a vivid reconstruction, with all the sights and smells of that magnificent dark-age settlement.

But it was not so much the morning as the early evening that had set me thinking about the many layers of time. For, before evensong in the Minster, a service which is itself a glorious thread of connection and continuity with the past, I had dipped down into the crypt, far deeper than the Coppergate diggings, where the remains of *Eboracum,* the Roman city, can be seen; and there I saw for myself the most sacred thing in York: a simple clay tablet from the first century, on which, 200 years before Constantine ever heard on the streets of York his call to empire, an anonymous Christian had scratched the chi-rho, the sign of Christ. That sign was made within living memory of the events of Easter, and uncovered only in our own time, in the very heart of England: the sign of our salvation.

I left York with the sense that there might also be signs

of hope, even in the layers of my own life, waiting to be rediscovered.

48

Early Rising

I am glad that there are now so many early-morning Easter services: pre-dawn vigils and fires, gatherings of Christians to greet the rising sun in the light of the Risen Son.

At least, in theory I'm glad. In practice, I find that I am not such an early riser as I would theoretically like to be, and that my drowsy and gradual coming-to, all my yawning and stretching, seem to take more effort, and, together with that essential first cup of tea in bed, seem to take longer than they used to.

But perhaps I am in good company. Many of us will read George Herbert's glorious poem 'Easter' on Easter Day. One way of reading the poem is to see it as Herbert's long, metrically intricate way of cajoling himself to get out of bed.

Easter day would have started for Herbert like every day, with early morning matins, and his poem 'Matins' opens with the line 'I cannot open mine eyes'. I know how he feels. Though, of course, Herbert goes on in the following lines to change the sense of the first line, because of Christ's transforming presence with him:

I cannot ope mine eyes,
But thou art ready there to catch
My morning-soul and sacrifice:
Then we must needs for that day make a match.

'Ah, you're already there in church ahead of me, I'd better get going and catch up,' he seems to be saying. But, as he crossed the little lane in Bemerton from the rectory to the church, still wiping the sleep from his eyes, and stumbled through Psalm 57, one of the proper psalms on an early Easter Day matins, Herbert might well have recited verse 9 with feeling: as a quite literal 'wake-up call':

Awake up, my glory, awake, lute and harp: I myself will awake right early

Certainly, it was that line which became the inspiration and starting point for 'Easter', whose first verse opens:

Rise heart; thy Lord is risen. Sing his praise
Without delayes,

And whose second verse echoes that with a call to his Lute:

Awake, my lute, and struggle for thy part
With all thy art.

But this Easter wake-up call differs from his poem 'Matins', in which we sense an effort to catch up with Christ, who is 'ready there', an effort all packed into those two words 'must needs'. But, in 'Easter', it is the Risen Christ himself who graciously comes to Herbert where he lies abed and actually helps him rise:

Rise heart; thy Lord is risen. Sing his praise
Without delayes,

Who takes thee by the hand, that thou likewise
With him mayst rise.

We are not far off that moment when, in his masterpiece 'Love (III)', Herbert will sum all this up in the simple phrase 'Love took my hand'.

So I intend to get up early on this particular Easter Morning. Like Herbert's lute, I might 'struggle for my part', but I also know that, when I stumble into church to celebrate an early Easter communion, Love will have risen before me and be ready to greet me, and I will say to him, as Herbert does in 'Easter':

I got me flowers to straw thy way;
I got me boughs off many a tree:
But thou wast up by break of day,
And brought'st thy sweets along with thee.

49

On Doing Nothing After Easter

I love the feel of the days after Easter: it's like bathing in a clear stream after climbing a high mountain, like floating on buoyant waters after laying down a heavy load.

For those who have been ministering in their churches over Holy Week, clergy and lay ministers alike, part of the load that they lay down is just the sheer intellectual, physical, and spiritual labour of planning, organising, and 'taking' the plethora of extra Holy Week services; the effort of writing and preaching those crucial sermons that take both preacher and congregation deep into the heart of our faith: its unflinching confrontation with the worst of human malice, the deepest of human grief, the strangest of human confusions, and then, after the eerie pause of Holy Saturday, the resurgence of joy, a joy that itself passes all understanding but that nevertheless we seek, Easter by Easter, to understand a little more.

No wonder so many pastors and church leaders spend the second half of Easter Day, and a good deal of Easter Monday, curled up in their beds in a kind of semi-comatose recovery position.

But that sense of relief, and the release that follows it, as we emerge into the classic clergy post-Easter break, is more than just relaxation after effort. If we have been able to hear even fragments of our own sermons, if we have taken in spiritually even a hint of what we took in bodily with our Easter communion, then there is a release from much heavier burdens than work, there are stronger arms than our own lifting us, and a hidden voice, that was always there, but overlaid by so much else, saying clearly at last: 'Come unto me, all ye who labour and are heavy laden, and I will give you rest.'

So, after the long wilderness journey of Lent, we come again to the spring and the source, and bathe in it. For me, it often feels like that transcendent moment in the Nicolas Roeg film *Walkabout*, where, after the desert journey, when they can scarcely move for thirst and heat, their aboriginal guide brings the children to a deep green pool, and there is a beautiful wordless sequence where they dive, and bathe, and swim in its refreshing blue-green waters.

The buoyant waters of the Easter season have probably carried many of us down from our own Easter mountain in many different directions, and to many different hideaways and boltholes. They have carried us, as they do most years, to north Norfolk, and a little cottage in Brancaster, where we have the pleasure of doing nothing for a week – nothing but floating on grace, paddling in its shallows, and sailing over its depths.

Even George and Zara, our two retired greyhounds, for whom this is the first Norfolk excursion, notice the difference. After six months of demonstrating to us daily how to loll on armchairs, snooze on sofas, and drape oneself elegantly over a chaise longue, they have noted, with approval, that we are finally getting the hang of it, and learning how to relax.

50

Found Poetry

I am a latecomer to the fascinating form of 'found poetry': the art of discerning the hidden traces of a poem amid a clutter of printed prose, or finding them strewn along the street in signs, or scattered on a map in place-names. It is the literary equivalent of the whole genre of art *trouvé*: the idea that one might find hidden beauties and meanings amid the everyday, amid the discarded, and that the art made from these 'found' things might itself send the beholder back into the world with new eyes and a new appreciation – an antidote to our throw-away culture.

My first effort at 'found poetry' came when I happened to notice what a beautiful sequence was made by the names of the last little fishing boats, remnants of the North Sea fishing fleet, tucked in to the harbour at Amble, in Northumbria. I saw those names early one morning, many years ago, picked out in fresh paint on the old wooden prows, jotted them down, and carried them around for years, like a jeweller with a pocketful of rare pearls waiting to find their right setting. Eventually, it came, and I wrote the poem 'Saying the Names' on the back of a shopping list, swaying on the upper deck of a bus, celebrating

> …The ancient names picked out in this year's paint:
> *Providence, Bold Venture, Star Divine*
> Are first along the quay-side. *Fruitful Bough*

Has stemmed the tides to bring her harvest in,
Orcadian Mist and *Sacred Heart*, *Aspire*,
Their names are numinous, a found poem.
Those Bible-burnished phrases live and lift
Into the brightening tide of morning light
And beg to be recited, chanted out,
For names are incantations, mysteries
Made manifest like ships on the horizon.
Eastward their long line tapers towards dawn
And ends at last with *Freedom*, *Radiant Morn*.

Later still, I came to that other kind of found poetry, where one glimpses the poem hidden in the midst of someone else's prose, like a shy deer hiding in a thicket.

This time it was the prose of C. S. Lewis. I was re-reading his trenchant and prophetic book *The Abolition of Man*. The first chapters are a sharp analysis of the way our present approach to science and technology is reducing both the world and its people to so much 'dead stuff' to be manipulated and exploited; but, in the final chapter, Lewis asks us to 'imagine a new natural philosophy' combining modern science with ancient reverence and respect.

And that is where I glimpsed the live deer in the thicket; for his prose lifts to his theme, and I found sentence after sentence quickened with the underlying music of iambic pentameter. My 'found poem', 'Imagine', involved no change to any of Lewis's phrases, just a little judicious selection and arrangement.

As we try to recover from the catastrophic effects of our

reductive and exploitative approach to nature, his words seem more vital than ever:

> Imagine a new natural philosophy;
> I hardly know what I am asking for;
> Far-off echoes, that primeval sense,
> With blood and sap, Man's pre-historic piety,
> Continually conscious, and continually …
> Alive, alive and growing like a tree
> And trees as dryads, or as beautiful,
> The bleeding trees in Virgil and in Spenser
> The tree of knowledge and the tree of life
> Growing together, that great ritual
> Pattern of nature, beauties branching out
> The cosmic order, ceremonial,
> Regenerate science, seeing from within …
>
> To participate is to be truly human.

'Saying the Names' and 'Imagine' are both collected in The Singing Bowl, *published by Canterbury Press.*

51

Bluebells

The bluebells are out at last, long-expected and yet still surprising, new, miraculous. They are sprinkled and scattered in strokes and splashes alongside the paths around college, as though just laid on by a fast-working Impressionist, painting *en plein air*.

But in the sloping woods on Rivey Hill above Linton, they are spread as a delicate carpet, a delicious shimmer of blue threaded through with the underlying greens and browns of the forest floor. These, surely, must be among 'the heaven's embroidered cloths' that Yeats wished he might have, and at the sight of them I draw in my breath and tread softly.

Even as I stand in this one particular wood, I imagine for a moment all the bluebells in all the woods of England: shimmering pools of blue wherein the souls of so many are treading softly with bare feet, as though they paddled in water. Even those who stand outwardly obdurate on the paths in their stout walking shoes are inwardly wading there and are refreshed.

What is it that gives bluebells their particular enchantment? It is not simply that they have been breathed into being by the long-awaited spring, and are harbingers of good things to come, that they are among the lovely lowly things that bring good news.

It is more than that: it is the colour itself; for it is the colour of the sky, suddenly come down to earth. When we look up into that enticing blue, it always escapes us, always recedes; it is everywhere and nowhere. However high we fly, the blue is always beyond us; but, here, in these secret scatterings and holy showings deep in the woods, that blue is on our level, beckoning us to look down as well as up, and to take off our shoes on holy ground. In that sense, they are a sign of incarnation, of that great descent of heaven itself to earth which began in Mary's womb. Perhaps that is why it is so fitting that she is always shown clothed in blue, and her annunciation comes in spring.

When I was coming out of a dark winter and walking abroad for the first time in many months, still on crutches and testing the mend of a badly broken leg, I walked the coastal path at Brancaster, and felt a healing touch in the blue of Norfolk's wide April skies, something I celebrated in my poem 'First Steps':

The April sun shines clear beyond your shelter
And clean as sight itself. The reed-birds sing,
As heaven reaches down to touch the earth
And circle her, revealing everywhere
A lovely, longed-for blue.
Breathe deep and be renewed by every breath,
Kinned to the keen east wind and cleansing air,
As though the blue itself were blowing through you.

But now, as April turns to May, I have that blue laid out at my feet, inviting me to touch it like the hem of Christ's garment. And, as I do just that, I realise something new: blue is not only the colour of heaven; it is also the colour of sorrow. The blue mood, the blue tone, the blues themselves that I sing and sometimes feel, are the very things taken up and redeemed when heaven came down to earth.

And now, amid the bluebells, looking down towards the village and its church tower, I hear another bell, summoning me to give thanks for all of this.

52

Top Dead Centre

One bright May morning, just before the *Church Times* Poetry Festival was kick-started into life and motion by Canon Mark Oakley, I was sitting outside Sarum College, contemplating the astonishing spire of Salisbury Cathedral.

The Cathedral Close, unlike some, is not actually close at all, but spread out at a leisurely distance from the cathedral itself, so that one can see the whole edifice without obstruction, and the great building has room to breathe, to show all its proportions, and to feed the imagination.

The eye is inevitably drawn upwards to the spire, as the broad spread and foundation of the cathedral, with all its walls and arches, narrows and rises into that slender arrow: a great sermon in stone finally coming to the point.

And the point, where the stone narrows to nothing and disappears into the blue, is, of course, a sign, a sign pointing away from itself and all its achievements, upwards towards something utterly transcendent.

But, suddenly, I saw it all the other way round. I saw the tip of the spire as the beginning, as though the whole building started there, with a little gift of being, from out of the blue, and grew downwards and outwards from that tiny point, down to the broad walls, the deep foundations and welcoming doors, the accessible place of human community.

I suppose the whole place, and the faith that brought it into being, can always be seen both ways, is always both a receiving from above and a building-up from below; and, for a moment, I could see the two directions, the two movements, alternating, reciprocating.

These days after Ascension are like that, too: a pause in the midst of that reciprocal motion, poised between the great upward movement of the ascension that brings the resurrection to completion and climax, and the wonderful downrush of power and prayer which is Pentecost. This in-between time is the upward equivalent of Holy Saturday, that other expectant pause at the lowest point, between the deepest downward descent of Christ into hell, and the great uprush of resurrection. But, for now, all that drives the wheel of the liturgical year is suspended and still, before the explosion of Pentecost sets it all in motion again. We rest for a moment at 'top dead centre', as the motorcycle mechanics like to say.

I once did an evening class in motorcycle maintenance, and the teacher patiently explained to me that, for any fine tuning and adjustment of the engine, you must first find top dead centre: that point when the upward travelling cylinder has come to the very top of its range, and so its reciprocal cylinder is at its lowest; that point of poise and compression just before the spark plug fires and the great expansion of gases powers the cylinder down again to set everything in motion.

My attempts to find the exact top dead centre always failed, and I gave up on that course after a term, which is why I am waiting now for my bike to be repaired by a professional; but I am very glad that the liturgical year always finds top dead centre for me, and I draw breath before *ergon*, the action, the energy, the urge that is within the word lit*urg*y, fires up again at Pentecost and gets us all moving.

53

Lists and Litanies

I have been luxuriating in the lush exuberance of late May. All my familiar walks, lovely as they were at the beginning of the month, are somehow richer, fuller still with bright yellow buttercups and fringes of the flowering hawthorn hedge, the luxuriant grasses by the river an even fresher green.

Once it was my greyhounds, George and Zara, nosing scents, who slowed me down, but now I delay them with my dawdling, my stopping to draw in breath at views that are everywhere breathtaking, fuller, and more luxuriant than they were the day before.

The May of 1819 was rich like this one, and I almost feel the presence of Leigh Hunt standing with me as I pause to gaze, for he put it all better than I can, seeing the very same things, and rising to his account of them in prose that lilts, even as it lists, and trembles on the brink of poetry:

The grass is in its greenest beauty, the young corn has covered the more naked fields; the hedges are powdered with snowy and sweet-scented blossoms of the hawthorn, as beautiful as myrtle flowers; the orchards give us trees, and the most lovely flowers at once; and the hedge-banks, woods and meadows, are sprinkled in profusion with cowslip, the wood-roof, the orchis, the blue gemander, the white anemone, the lilly of the valley … and when the vital sparkle of the day is over, in sight and sound, the nightingale still continues to tell us of its joy.

If these words from *The Calendar of Nature*, published on 9 May, came to the brink of poetry, they did much more than that. Fortunately for us, they reached Hunt's young friend John Keats, who read them just at the beginning of his *annus mirabilis*, and that same month, transmuting Hunt's prose, and so much more, into his golden verse, he wrote the 'Ode to a Nightingale'.

Keats takes up the rich theme almost where Hunt leaves off, at sunset, and it is all the richer for being sensed intensely at night. Hunt's list is now a litany:

> I cannot see what flowers are at my feet,
> Nor what soft incense hangs upon the boughs,
> But, in embalmed darkness, guess each sweet
> Wherewith the seasonable month endows
> The grass, the thicket, and the fruit-tree wild;
> White hawthorn, and the pastoral eglantine;
> Fast fading violets cover'd up in leaves;
> And mid-May's eldest child,
> The coming musk-rose, full of dewy wine …

The sheer abundance and profusion, the extravagant, generous overflow of nature in this month is more 'seasonable' still for those of us who keep the liturgical calendar alongside Hunt's 'Calendar of Nature'.

The long expected and still overflowing abundance of Pentecost suits with the season. The apostles were not drunk on new wine, but on something headier still, as Keats, too, turned from his 'draft of vintage, full of the warm south' to the stronger stuff of poetry.

Like Hunt and Keats, St Luke finds himself compelled, by sheer abundance, to chant a list: this time, a list of all the nations, the rich and varied tongues into which the Spirit poured the rich wine of the gospel:

Parthians, Medes, Elamites, and residents of Mesopotamia, Judaea and Cappadocia, Pontus and Asia, Phrygia and Pamphylia, Egypt and the parts of Libya belonging to Cyrene, and visitors from Rome, both Jews and proselytes, Cretans and Arabs.

There's a poem in there somewhere!

54

Happiness

There is great pleasure in turning again, after a long interval, to a book that was formative in your youth. The book seems fresh and new; yet at the same time you find, on page after page, expressions and ideas that are so much a part of your life that you had forgotten where they came from.

I have had that pleasure in re-reading *The Importance of Living*, a collection of essays and translations from Chinese by Lin Yutang, a twentieth-century Chinese writer, translator, and philosopher. I read this book in my early twenties, and it was my first taste of Taoist classics such as the *Tao Te Ching*, with its gentle wisdom drawn from observing and imitating the flow of water.

Yutang's own essays are wonderful, too: little meditations-in-the-moment on the pleasures of lying in bed, drinking tea, smoking, and watching clouds. Every page enhances one's appreciation of everyday things, of hidden beauties, of 'heaven in ordinary'. He quotes later Chinese classics, too, one of which, by the seventeenth-century writer Chin Shengt'an, is called *Thirty-three Happy Moments*. Some are very simple, like this one: 'To cut with a big sharp knife a bright green watermelon on a big scarlet plate of a summer afternoon. Ah, is this not happiness?'

Some celebrate moments of release and charity, such as the one in which Chin describes taking out from a trunk some dozens of IOUs that he knew people could not or would not repay. He writes: 'I put them together in a pile and make a bonfire of them and I look up at the sky and see the last trace of smoke disappear. Ah, is this not happiness?'

And so often, for him, as for me, the happy moments are associated with the presence or the memory of flowing water: 'To hear our children recite the classics so fluently, like the sound of water pouring from a vase. Ah, is this not happiness?'

Or when he hears young people singing Soochow folk songs as they tread a waterwheel and writes: 'The water comes up over the wheel in a gushing torrent, like molten silver or melting snow. Ah, is this not happiness?'

This book also gave me my first love of Chinese poetry, and I went on from it to read Arthur Waley's beautiful limpid translations. I was fascinated by the creative miracle of translation itself; for Chinese and English are so different, and their poetic traditions, and techniques, are so distinct, and yet, somehow, meaning and beauty can flow between the two languages.

I had taken up the book out of a vague premonition that I needed its wisdom again, needed to pause, to reflect, to appreciate. And then came a lovely moment of synchronicity. Out of the blue, I received an email from a Chinese poet in the United States proposing to translate 51 of my sonnets for a Chinese edition, with a parallel text, and asking me to write a special preface for it.

I returned to the pages of Yutang with a quiet delight, and imagined, for a moment, what it would be like to see my lines transformed into the beautiful characters of the Chinese language, whose ideograms are both pictures and poetry. Ah, is this not happiness?

55

A Faded Photograph

Once again it is the time of year when time itself gradually intensifies for our students. I feel it even as I pass under the Gothic arch of our gatehouse tower; I sense the pressure and concentration as stressed-out undergraduates pass me in the corridor and scurry off, book-laden, to libraries and study rooms.

In most colleges, this intensity deepens and darkens for the next week or so, until it passes through the black hole of Tripos exams itself and emerges, on the other side, in an explosion of fireworks, feasting, and celebration through May Week.

But, in Girton, there is a special celebration offered on this side of the Tripos-horizon, and for a good reason. The College Feast commemorates Cambridge's long-delayed admission of women to degrees; and the 70th anniversary this year has coincided with the 100th anniversary of giving some women the vote. The feast is always held *before* Tripos, and no one wears a gown, as a gesture of solidarity with all those generations of women who did the work and took the exams, but were never given degrees.

But just outside the hall in which the feast is kept is a poignant Victorian photograph. Taken in 1891, it shows a group of Girton students in the grounds of the college, with its Gothic towers and turrets in the background, all of them fully robed and gowned, some wearing or carrying mortarboards, the signs and insignia of everything that they were being denied. They were members of the newly formed Dramatic Society, giving a performance of *The Princess*, Tennyson's thought-provoking medley, published 40 years earlier, a fantasy about the founding of a women's college.

Indeed, the debates in Victorian society which *The Princess* provoked may well have contributed to the changes of heart and mind which led to the actual founding of colleges for women. And Tennyson's imaginary college, half castle, half cloister, almost certainly influenced Alfred Waterhouse when he gave Girton its Gothic arches, and all its little fairytale towers and turrets.

So those early students had the perfect setting for their dramatic reading. I look closely at their clear, intelligent faces, and wonder with what sense of irony, subversion, prophecy, and bravado they donned those gowns. I sometimes wish that I could summon some sound from the faded sepia on our wall and hear in what tones, and with what hopes, they proclaimed Lilia's lines from near the beginning of the poem:

> Quick answered Lilia 'There are thousands now
> Such women, but convention beats them down:
> It is but bringing up; no more than that:
> You men have done it: how I hate you all!
> Ah, were I something great! I wish I were
> Some mighty poetess, I would shame you then,
> That love to keep us children! O I wish
> That I were some great princess, I would build
> Far off from men a college like a man's,
> And I would teach them all that men are taught;
> We are twice as quick!' And here she shook aside
> The hand that played the patron with her curls.

Lilia's twenty-first-century sisters are still having, all too often, to 'shake aside the hand that plays the patron', but there has nevertheless been some real progress from that day to this. If I long to hear again the sounds sealed in that silent photograph, I also sometimes wish that we could give those early students a glimpse of graduation now.

56

Coleridge in Highgate

One Saturday morning, I found myself climbing Highgate Hill, pausing to catch my breath just at the spot where Andrew Marvell's cottage used to be, and then pressing doggedly on, up past the elegant reading rooms of the wonderfully named Highgate Literary and Scientific Institution, and on at last to St Michael's, a Neo-Gothic church built in the last years of Coleridge's life, whose dedication he attended, and where his body is now laid to rest.

That body has been in the news recently, as his coffin was rediscovered during restoration work, interred in part of an old wine cellar. The papers, as you can imagine, had a field day, *The Guardian* leading with: 'It probably wouldn't have surprised his long-suffering friends, but the remains of the poet Samuel Taylor Coleridge have been rediscovered in a wine cellar.'

While it is true that there were times when Sara Coleridge, who is buried alongside the poet, did have some trouble keeping her husband out of 'Inns and Pot-houses': in fact, in his last days, when he became known as the 'sage of Highgate', it was eloquence, clarity of vision, and a profound insight into how we are all included and constantly renewed in the creative life of the Holy Trinity that really lifted his spirits.

Indeed, I was visiting St Michael's to give a talk on Coleridge as a Christian thinker: part of a whole day called 'Reclaim the Crypt', raising funds for a proper restoration and memorial to mark his resting place. Many of the present-day Coleridge family were there, in some of whom something of the poet's own features, living and breathing again, could be seen, and in all of whom there seemed to be a genuine sense of the genius and the suffering, the insight and the faith, of their great ancestor.

There was much to be enjoyed that day: lectures, dramatic readings, and new musical settings of famous poetic passages. But the heart of it came at the end, in a prayerful rededication of the memorial stone whose epitaph Coleridge himself had composed, which begins 'Stop, Christian passer-by! Stop, Child of God … O, lift one thought in prayer for S. T. C.' And stop we did. The Vicar, the Revd Olakunle Ayodeji, read out the epitaph, then paused and allowed a rich silence to fill the church. After so many words, the silence was full, replete, and I thought of those lines in the *Mariner:*

> No voice; but oh! The silence sank
> Like music on my heart.

In that deep silence, I also remembered how I had come to this church, many years before, and had been moved, standing before that stone, to compose a sonnet expressing something of my own debt to the great poet:

> Stop, Christian passer-by! – Stop, child of God!
> You made your epitaph imperative,
> And stopped this wedding guest! But I am glad
> To stop with you and start again, to live
> From that pure source, the all-renewing stream,
> Whose living power is imagination,

And know myself a child of the I AM,
Open and loving to his whole creation.

Your glittering eye taught mine to pierce the veil,
To let his light transfigure all my seeing,
To serve the shaping Spirit whom I feel,
And make with him the poem of my being.
I follow where you sail towards our haven,
Your wide wake lit with glimmerings of heaven.

57

Willow

I have at last rescued *Willow* from where she languished under tarpaulins in a muddy field, spruced her up, and launched her again on the Great Ouse. *Willow* is my lovely little replica of the 'Rob Roy' sailing canoe.

John 'Rob Roy' MacGregor was one of those eccentric Victorian explorers whose exploits are still celebrated – indeed, some claim that he invented the sport of canoeing. But his way was not competitive: instead, he revelled in individual freedom and a desire to see as much of God's good earth as possible.

Having seen birch-bark canoes in Canada, he came home to design and build his own little canoe: slender, clinker-built, with cedar decks and a stepping place for a light mast and single sail. My *Willow* follows his original lines, but, in truth, looks more like a smaller version of the light Elven boats in *The Lord of the Rings* than anything from *The Last of the Mohicans.*

MacGregor didn't just paddle and sail: he wrote. And the vivid account of his adventures, published in 1866 as *A Thousand Miles in the Rob Roy Canoe*, was an overnight sensation. On the opening page, he praises the life and prowess of the canoeist thus:

> He can steer within an inch in a narrow place, and can easily pass through reeds and weeds, or branches and grass; can work his sail without changing his seat; can

shove with his paddle when aground, and can jump out in good time to prevent a bad smash. He can wade and haul his craft over shallows, or drag it on dry ground, through fields and hedges, over dykes, barriers, and walls; can carry it by hand up ladders and stairs, and can transport his canoe over high mountains.

I have to say, this is all rather too athletic for me: I turn to sail and stream for drifting and ease. Of course, MacGregor praises that, too:

You lean all the time against a swinging backboard, and when the paddle rests on your lap you are at ease as in an armchair; so that, while drifting along with the current or the wind, you can gaze around, and eat or read, or sketch, or chat with the starers on the bank.

That's more my style. And so I have relaunched *Willow* and found a place to keep her where I have easier access to the river, and where it's broad enough for me to have some fun with *Willow*'s little red sail.

MacGregor was a devout Christian with a social conscience, a philanthropist, involved in the Ragged School movement and other charities. But he never draws the links that one might expect between the gospel and his chosen mode of adventure.

For me, though, to be borne afloat on water, to love and study its grace and movement, to sense the smallest zephyr and hoist one's sails to it, steering with whatever skill one has but content to be borne before the breeze and take the adventure that comes … all this bodies forth so much of what the gospel tells of the Spirit: free as the wind, refreshing and life-giving as the stream.

It takes a lifetime to be 'born again of water and the Spirit', but a little of that lifetime, carried along visibly by the grace of water and wind, might help with the inward and spiritual journey.

58

Church Fetes

The season of fêtes and garden parties is well and truly on us: bunting is going up on village greens and over lych-gates, churches are made festive with flowers, and time-worn tombolas are set spinning again.

I really enjoy church fêtes. I like them for their ordinariness, for their sense of make-do and mend, for the wonderful variety of ages, sizes, and shapes of the people who attend them – so different from the wall-to-wall photo-shopped images of youth and glamour that assail us, and ultimately oppress us, in the world of advertising, where every lawn is perfectly trimmed, every couple young and beautiful, and every family well turned out and perfectly happy.

At a church fête, by contrast, everyone comes just as they are. We assemble much as the worn-out household items and well-thumbed paperbacks are assembled for the bric-a-brac stall: people take us as they find us.

And the children, who all have access at home to highly sophisticated computer games created with a budget of millions, suddenly discover that they are just as happy kicking a football through target holes cut into a plywood board, or fishing with a stick and string for yellow plastic ducks in a tub of water.

In fact, at Linton, we take it a stage further and have a 'duck race', launching a whole flotilla of plastic ducks, each 'sponsored' or purchased for fund-raising, and let them float down the Granta as it curves round the church, and wait with bated breath to see which is first to float under the Lady Bridge. The real ducks, and Mussolini the goose, look on in amazement.

And, again, everything runs happily counter to the oppressive worldliness of a consumer society. Here, nobody cares who wins; here, we are glad to bid in the auction for more than a thing is worth; here, we are just as happy when the thrown hoop misses as when it settles over a bottle, which will almost certainly find its way back on to the stall next year.

Here, we celebrate the old and familiar rather than insisting on the shiny and new, and yet there is a newness, too: old acquaintances renewed, newcomers to the parish suddenly feeling that they belong, a new thankfulness that all of this is still going on. If a scribe of the Kingdom is like the householder who takes out of his treasury things old and things new, then perhaps there's something of that hidden Kingdom in every church fête.

Even Philip Larkin emerges from his wry melancholy to celebrate these home-brewed affairs. His wonderful poem 'Show Saturday' was written about a county show in Bellingham in 1973, rather than a church fête, but it notices and savours many of the same sights:

> Bead-stalls, balloon-men ... a beer-marquee that
> Half-screens a canvas Gents; a tent selling tweed,
> And another, jackets. Folks sit about on bales
> Like great straw dice ...

And that poem rises to a powerful recognition that, even in

the ordinariness of these occasions, we can discern
      ... much greater gestures; something they share
      That breaks ancestrally each year into
      Regenerate union. Let it always be there.

I can only say Amen.

59

Making Hay

They were making hay, up in the small fields, traced out with their dry-stone walls on the sun-soaked slopes of Swaledale, on the hottest day of the year.

I watched a tractor, tiny like a toy in the distance, pulling its mower back and forth across the walled field, and another, doing just the same, in the opposite direction, in the field below.

Maggie and I had walked down from Arkengarthdale into the village of Reeth, and sat at a table outside the Black Bull. I nursed my pint of Old Peculier, engaged in that most relaxing of all pastimes: watching other people work.

The two little tractors plying back and forth were far enough away to be inaudible, and their gentle criss-crossing was at once hypnotic and soothing, though I imagined the farmers themselves, casting a backward glance at their tracks and breathing the air full of dust and grass-cuttings, must have been feeling the heat. I guessed that by day's end they'd be down this way and glad of a pint of OP themselves.

I found myself recalling Hilaire Belloc's classic essay 'The Mowing of a Field', although that was set in another era, the last days of the scythe, and not in the Yorkshire Dales, but in a hidden valley in Belloc's beloved Sussex.

His essay celebrates the art of mowing with a scythe in wonderful and intricate detail, and yet every detail somehow rings out, becomes universal, celebrates every good art and craft. So, first, he sharpens his scythe, just as a poet might hone his or her mind for the muse:

First, the stone clangs and grinds against the iron harshly; then it rings musically to one note; then, at last, it purrs as though iron and stone were exactly suited … and I, when I heard it in that June dawn, with everything quite silent except the birds, let down the scythe and bent myself to mow.

'The good mower', he remarks, 'goes forward very steadily, his scythe-blade just barely missing the ground, every grass falling; the swish and rhythm of his mowing are always the same.'

Of course, it makes him think of poetry: 'The pen thinks for you; and so does the scythe mow for you if you treat it honourably.' And so, in turn, that deep almost unconscious rhythm makes him think of prayer:

In this mowing should be like one's prayers – all of a sort and always the same, and so made that you can establish a monotony and work them, as it were, with half your mind: that happier half, the half that does not bother.

Naturally, the cut grass, and the scythe itself, must bring to mind our mortality: 'The days of man are but as grass; for he flourisheth as a flower of the field. For as soon as the wind goeth over it, it is gone; and the place thereof shall know it no more.'

But, somehow, Belloc, who had a stronger sense than most both of mortality and melancholy, lifts it all into beauty, and, finally, into fellowship. He finds a companion in his mowing, and brings out a jar of small ale to share with him.

Savouring my own pint in the heat of the day, I remembered his little saying: 'Small ale goes well with mowing.'

60

The Temple of Peace

I have a little hut at the bottom of the garden, which is called (more in hope than expectation) the Temple of Peace. I borrowed the name from Gladstone, for in any house he inhabited, that was the name he gave to his study. Not that my little hexagonal hut, which is, to be honest, no more than a glorified gazebo, would stand comparison with the spacious rooms, well-stocked bookshelves and lovely big desks which furnished the various 'Temples of Peace' enjoyed by the Grand Old Man. Nevertheless, I remember how pleased I was with that hut, with its comfortable chair, small writing table, rack for my pipes and, pinned on the wall, a poem of Wendell Berry's called 'How to Be a Poet', with its wonderful opening lines:

> Make a place to sit down.
> Sit down. Be quiet.
> You must depend upon
> affection, reading, knowledge,
> skill – more of each
> than you have –

I even went so far as to intimate to my friends that this hut was to be 'my trysting place with the muse'.

However, this was news to her. For the first few times I sat solemnly in the writing hut, pen in hand, entirely at her disposal, I found that she had booked the day off, or perhaps just pulled a sickie. There was nothing doing. In fact, the first poem that came to me after I had built the temple, came fully, clearly, eagerly waiting to be written, and very suddenly, while I was on a crowded train, and I ended up writing it down with a biro on the front of the paper bag I had for my packed lunch.

But even as I did so I had an obscure feeling that the Temple of Peace had something to do with it, that somehow by creating that external space where I waited in silence and in vain, I had opened a new inner space for the poem that came to me on the crowded train. Perhaps my muse was glad I had made and kept a space for her, even though on this occasion she had loftily disdained to use it. Perhaps the Temple was honoured and fecund even when it was empty.

I have found that to be true in other ways and places too, that the making and keeping of spaces in our outer lives somehow clears paths and opens spaces in our inner lives. The lovely mediaeval church in our village of Linton stands empty most of the time, as I suppose do most of the parish churches of England, and yet it too holds something open, something about presence and purpose, but also something about peace and silence which is, I cannot help feeling, as richly available and strangely efficacious for those who glance at it and hurry past, as for those who open the door and drink in what it has to offer. The whole village, both outwardly and inwardly, would feel different if that Temple wasn't there. I wonder if that prayer-shaped space still shapes the prayers of those for whom the occasional visit is only a memory, as well as for those who often go there, outwardly and visibly, to keep tryst with the invisible.

61

A Little Pamphlet

I have in my hands a little pamphlet, printed on thick, cream-coloured paper, its borders brown and faded, but the beautiful letterpress of the lines on its cover as clear as ever:

Words and Verses spoken in the Garden of Bemerton Rectory, near Salisbury, in the afternoon of Tuesday June 6th, 1933.

And on the inside of that cover, in pencil, is a signed note from the author of those words:

For Charles and Janet Ashbee, from John Masefield. Christmas 1933

Just holding the pamphlet makes me feel as though I were there in George Herbert's garden, gathered with the then Poet Laureate John Masefield and his friends on the 300th anniversary of Herbert's death, as they breathed his poems afresh into the summer air.

Masefield, in his remarks, seems as much enamoured of the man as of the poetry and he draws as much on *The Country Parson* as on the poems themselves. Most of what he says is taken from Walton's famous 'Life of Herbert' but he gives one strikingly original insight, which I have never seen anywhere else. Perhaps knowing that Herbert himself loved and collected proverbs, Masefield draws on an American proverb for insight into Herbert's life and work, and says:

There is a very good American proverb. I know not who made it … 'When lifting, get underneath'. I have often thought of it, and I think of it now as the secret of George Herbert's power upon men. He did not pour unction from above, he wound down into the hearts of his parishioners and built a foundation there, wooing each heart to each truth, explaining and giving beauty to each rule and rite, and making it significant to his hearers, persuading them of it all, till none could have held away.

This gets right to the heart of Herbert's own poetic mastery, but it also gets to the heart of his Master, and if Herbert had known this proverb I think he would have applied it, in a poem, to Christ himself. For the whole self-emptying of Christ in the incarnation, and even more in the passion, and the descent into hell, is the tale of how God does not give unction or instruction from above, but comes down into our humanity, *gets underneath* with us, underneath the weight and the burden, lifting it in us and with us and for us. It is not above, but underneath, that we feel, in their strength, the everlasting arms.

The pamphlet came to me as a gift from a friend, who is the grandson of the man to whom Masefield wrote the dedication. He enclosed a brief note for me saying 'I feel this little curio ought to be in the hands of a poet in Herbert's tradition, so I hope you will accept it'.

I was glad indeed to accept it and am glad to belong to that tradition, however distant in time and talent from Herbert himself. But holding this lovely leaflet, with all its history, I felt closer. To have such a thing in one's hands is to receive something that will never come from an ebook or a flat screen.

So once more I lift the little pamphlet from my desk, touching its creamy paper, and find myself, in Heaney's telling phrase, 'gleaning the unsaid off the palpable'.

62

Procrastination

I am a master of the art of procrastination. The more urgent a task is, the more I want to postpone it, and those occasions when I have neatly re-shelved my books, or even tidied my study, are all testament to how desperately I wanted to avoid the actual task in hand.

If you're looking for distraction, there is an entertaining little book called *The Art of Procrastination: A Guide to Effective Dawdling, Lollygagging and Postponing*. But it's more than just one of those jokey books kept on bookshop counters to tempt you while you're making your more serious purchase, for its author, John Perry, is a Professor of Philosophy at Stanford, and in among his many amusing accounts of postponement he makes some serious points. The chief of these is that, in spite of their reputation for idleness, procrastinators are often very productive. This 'Paradox of Procrastination', as he calls it, arises from the fact that in order to avoid whatever they perceive as 'Task A', the thing they are dutifully bound to do, procrastinators immediately take up something else, 'Task B', with great alacrity. But quite often 'Task B' produces something wonderful: a poem, a play, an inspired bit of scientific tinkering or thinking, in which the natural gifts of the procrastinator, unstressed by a sense of obligation, suddenly find creative release. This was certainly true of Coleridge, who threw off the *Ancient Mariner* as a kind of escape from his Big Project, which was to be an epic poem about the nature and origin of evil, followed by six odes, one on each of the four elements and one each on the sun and the moon. Coleridge spent the rest of his life berating himself for his abject failure to produce this great epic and these major odes, but of course, as every reader, except the poet, knew, *The Ancient Mariner* is his immortal epic on the problem of evil and includes a poetic celebration of the four elements and of the sun and the moon.

This isn't to say that everything we do to avoid 'Task A' is always quite so good. Sharpening pencils, arranging pens, and of course scrolling through Facebook and Twitter, can all seem appealing as 'displacement activities'. While deadlines concentrate the mind, they also make every distraction more alluring. Suppose a man were sitting down, finally, to write his weekly column. He might suddenly be tempted to reorganize his desk and then to write a Meredithian sonnet about it, like this:

Preliminary Ritual

First there is the clearing of the desk,
Displacing chaos for a working space,
And then the putting of each thing in place:
The pen and paper, ready for the task.
And then there is the opening of the pen,
The lifting of its lovely silver cap,
Which fits back on the barrel with a snap
Leaving the golden nib exposed. And then
With pen in hand you try a line or two
On scrap paper, you have a little go
To test how well both thought and ink might flow,

Hoping to find that both are coming through.
And so they are, but both are poor and thin,
Will they be turned aside by this harsh age?
Your pen is poised above the empty page
There's nothing for it now, but to begin.

63

An Icon

I was present at the service in which a new icon which 'Ikon John' Coleman has given the Retreat Association was hallowed. It was featured in the *Church Times* and shows the encounter between Jesus and the woman at the well. She stands, mantled in green, her empty water jar in one hand, the other gesturing away from her, perhaps towards the well, perhaps towards Christ himself, for he is numinously present just on the other side of the well, seated, in an earth-brown robe and a mantle blue as the heavens, one hand held towards his heart and set already in the sign of blessing, the other extended almost playfully towards the well, touching and swirling the water itself, gently, with his fingertips. Behind Christ, on the edge of the icon we can see his disconcerted and disapproving disciples, returning from their shopping trip, shocked to see Jesus welcoming so tainted and marginal a person as a Samaritan woman, but behind the woman we see, emerging from the city, a crowd who will become, through her ministry, a new Christian community.

I was with the Retreat Association as poet-in-residence for their triennial retreat in Swanwick, and the dedication of the icon was the conclusion of three days on the theme of 'sounding the silence', a paradoxical challenge for a poet, but I did my best to follow Wendell Berry's advice and to

> make a poem that does not disturb
> the silence from which it came.

As the icon was brought into our midst in that final service I reflected on how appropriate this particular image was for the Retreat Association. The story begins with exhaustion, stress, and rejection, and ends with a series of wonderful, paradoxical transformations and renewals: Jesus is exhausted at the well, sharing the exhaustion of the world, all the frustration and futility of our living, yet he is also the *fons et origo*, the well and spring of all renewal, and is able to offer this stranger the fountain of his own eternal life welling up within her. The woman is isolated and shunned by her community, which is why she comes to the well at noon and not in the cool of the morning or evening with the other women. She sees nothing but problems and barriers at first: the divisions of race and religion, the practical problem of the deep well, of having no buckets, and then the living presence of Jesus changes everything.

We see him through the icon, with one hand on his heart and the other on the water, himself the living connection between the two. Gazing at the icon, we see that the living water is already at the brim of the well. Has his presence drawn it up from the depths, or is it in fact flowing from him into the well and not the other way round? Certainly everything is reversed for the woman, and she who had to walk away from her village to find an outer source of refreshment will soon be herself a centre of renewal and be sharing good news in community.

After the service I sat by the little lake at Swanwick, dragonflies darted over above it like tiny threads of the blue sky itself come down to bless us, and I knelt to touch the water.

64

A New Word

Every so often one comes upon a new word and is entirely delighted with it, and happily this is an experience that goes on after those heady childhood years when, having dabbled in the shallows of babbling and baby talk, one launches out into the deep of reading and being read to, and delicious new words come flooding in to refresh and enrich the meadows of one's mind. I can still remember the moment, as a very young child, when my mother read me *The Tale of the Flopsy Bunnies*, and I first heard the word 'soporific':

> It is said that the effect of eating too much lettuce is soporific. I have never felt sleepy after eating lettuces; but then I am not a rabbit.

I didn't have to ask my mother what the new word meant because I could see from the next sentence that it meant 'making you feel sleepy' and I took great pleasure in using my new 'grown up' word and showing it off to my friends, casually remarking 'We sometimes have cocoa before bedtime because its so soporific!'

I read an article once saying that the text of *Flopsy Bunnies* should be changed because children's books should have a 'graded vocabulary' and 'soporific' was too advanced a word for young children and might put them off reading! On the contrary, all children love strange and mysterious words, as Lewis Carroll found out long ago.

But just this year, at the age of sixty, I had that same thrill of a new word, that I used to have at six! My new word was 'Ekphrastic', from a Greek term meaning to speak out or describe, and it's a term that has come specifically to mean the use of words to describe a work of art, and is now used to denote a whole genre known as 'Ekphrastic Poetry', a long tradition running from Homer's description of the shield of Achilles, to W. H. Auden's famous description, in *Musee Des Beaux Arts,* of Brueghel's *Landscape with the Fall of Icarus.* I only discovered what Ekphrastic poetry was when I was already in the middle of practising it! I have been commissioned by the American painter Bruce Herman to write a series of poems to go with a set of portraits he is painting called 'Ordinary Saints'. I had started to search for other poems about painting, to give me some idea of how this might be done, and stumbled happily upon a whole tradition of which I was unaware and a new word to go with it.

It's a fascinating discipline, to sit down before a picture which has already 'painted a thousand words', to draw from it, and give back to it, a few of the many hours of close attention and insight which the artist has already lavished upon it. For in all good paintings, there is excess, an over-plus, a quality of 'moreness' which no single viewing can ever exhaust. I discovered in the first poem in my sequence, about a portrait of the artist's father, and wrote:

> He meets us here, at home in his own skin,
> Which holds more colours than the eye can trace,

More substance, more humanity and grace
Than paint on wood can possibly contain,
All in the clarity of his kind face.

65

An Old Bridge

I've had a lovely day sailing, paddling, but mostly drifting in
Willow, my little sailing canoe. She has delicate lines and is
light on the water, and I take pleasure in the contrast with the
much bigger, heavier motorboats in whose wash she dances
disdainfully. She is named from some lines I love to chant
from *The Lady of Shallot* (and so restore their enchantment):

> By the margin, willow veil'd,
> Slide the heavy barges trail'd
> By slow horses; and unhail'd
> The shallop flitteth silken-sail'd
> Skimming down to Camelot:

T. S. Eliot said that Tennyson had the finest ear of all the poets
for the music inherent in the English language and you certainly hear it in 'The shallop flitteth silken-sail'd'. It's a pleasure just to say those words, and a lovely turn of Tennyson's
to recover and share the distinct word 'shallop': a seventeenth
century term for a shallow-drafted boat moved by sail and oar.
There is poetry not only in the sound but also in the contrast
between the heavy barge, trailed by its slow horses, and the
light shallop, flitting and skimming with the wind in its silken
sails.

Sadly, there are no slow horses trailing barges now, but my
little *Willow* certainly flits and skims, though today I was not
skimming down to Camelot, but up to St Ives.

The Huntingdonshire St Ives is a fine little town on the banks of the Great Ouse with a remarkable mediaeval bridge, one of only four in England still to be crowned, on its central arch, with a chapel.

It is especially beautiful as you approach it from the river (more so if you are in a silken-sailed shallop, rather than a heavy motorboat) and as you sail closer you notice another strange feature: the arches on each side of the bridge are different: four of them are the original gothic arches, but the last two, beyond the chapel, spanning to the old London road, are later rounded arches. This difference is witness to the tragedy of the English Civil War, but also to healing and recovery. When Cromwell's troops held the town in 1645 they partly blew up the bridge, destroying two of the southern arches, and installed a drawbridge instead, to defend the town from the Royalists. When peace returned, the bridge was rebuilt with two new arches in the more modern rounded style.

As I sailed gently towards it I found myself reflecting that it was no bad emblem for our own troubled times, for a country at odds with itself and its neighbours, for a time when many bridges and lines of communication are being broken and thrown down. In the end we will always need the bridges back, and somehow we will find a way of building them again. They will be different, they will have new tales to tell, but they will still be bridges. After all, this quintessentially English Town was named for St Ivo, a reputedly Persian bishop, and its bridge chapel dedicated, in 1426, to St Leger, a Burgundian Martyr. We are all more connected than we think.

I left *Willow* at the Town Quay and went to say a prayer in the bridge chapel, giving thanks for that other great Bridge between heaven and earth, which God founded in Christ, and which no power on earth can destroy.

66

Shed-fever

'I must go down to the shed again', I found myself sighing. Somehow my loftily named 'Temple of Peace', the little writing-hut which I have described earlier has ended up being referred to simply as 'the shed', or occasionally, with more dignity, 'the hut'. And somehow, 'life, the universe and everything' had been getting in the way and I hadn't been down there for over a week.

I realize that the musings in this book may sometimes give the impression that most of my life is spent reflecting in the quiet nooks of cathedral cites, walking my dogs in beautiful bluebell woods, and composing sonnets in the Temple of Peace. I only wish it were. These pages are testament to many delightful interludes, but, as in the building of any life, there are, in between the corners, some long dull walls of drudgery and duty, and, cluttering all one's living space, the usual stress-laden accumulation of unanswered emails, insoluble pastoral problems, and pressing publisher's deadlines. It's easy for poetry to get squeezed out, and that's why I sighed and said aloud, to no one in particular, 'I must go down to the shed again'. But even as I did so I had a distinct memory of my father, hard-pressed then as I am now, by academia, pastoralia, and unanswered correspondence, sighing, and saying with a far-away look in his eyes:

'I must go down to the sea again, the lonely sea and the sky.'

And if my mother were there, and heard him say it, she would immediately join in and say:

'And all I ask is a tall ship and a star to steer her by.'

And together they'd chant, to my amusement and amazement:

'And the wheel's kick and the wind's song and the white sail's shaking,
And a grey mist on the sea's face, and a grey dawn breaking.'

I sometimes think that just reciting Masefield's *Sea-Fever* did them almost as much good as sailing itself, though happily we all enjoyed some real sailing too, and that was the time when my father was really relaxed and happy, when he took us down to our little boat, *The Amaranth*, and we cast off, and hoisted sail.

That memory made me take my own sighing a little more seriously, so I closed up the laptop, put down the iPhone, and headed for the shed. Perhaps the shade of Masefield himself was following me, with my mother's well-worn copy of *Salt-Water Ballads*, for even as I closed the door, settled into my chair, and opened up my manuscript book, I found this little verse had formed in my mind. I suppose I had better call it 'Shed-fever':

I must go down to the shed again, the lonely shed and the den,
And all I ask is a kindly muse, and a hand to guide my pen,
And the verse-kick, and the vowel-song, and the words, warm and willing,

And a quiet time, and a full rhyme, and the white page fill-
ing.

67

An Apology for Idlers

Many years ago I picked up a scruffy edition of R. L. Stevenson's *Virginibus Puerisque*, from the bargain bin outside a second hand bookshop. Its worn covers, and the dogged ears of its pages, festooned with finger smudges and the occasional proprietorial red stamp, all proclaimed that it was an old school book, and that set me wondering. How ever did anyone come to think of setting *Virginibus Puerisque* as a school textbook? Perhaps they were misled by the title which, after all, proclaims that the book is written 'for girls and boys', perhaps the fact that the title is in Latin led someone to think that it was a solemn, learned, classical tome designed to inculcate into children all the prudent maxims of the old school: sobriety and industry, conformity, decency and decorum. If so, then they had clearly never read the text itself, for almost all the wonderful essays in this book are written with a gleeful energy whose entire purpose is to subvert the copybook maxims, the dictates of convention and the sage advice of our elders and betters. The great central essay is of course 'An Apology for Idlers'. Imagine a schoolchild, confined to class on a fine summer's day, being set to work to précis this essay! Here under the very nose of the teacher, a child's own inner thoughts are given clear expression:

> It is surely beyond doubt that people should be a good deal idle in youth ... If you look back on your own education, I'm sure it will not be the full, vivid, instructive hours of truantry that you will regret; you would rather

cancel some lacklustre periods between sleep and waking in the class.

And then there is the description of the pleasures of truantry itself, one of which I indulged in as a truant, and remains a pleasure to me now:

> He may pitch on some tuft of lilacs over a burn and smoke innumerable pipes to the tune of the water in the stones. A bird will sing in the thicket. And there he may fall into a vein of kindly thought, and see things in a new perspective.

Stevenson goes on to imagine an encounter between the idler and some bustling Mr Worldly Wiseman who demands what lesson they are learning. The idler replies:

> I lie here, by this water, to learn by root-heart a lesson which my master teaches me to call Peace, or Contentment.

Of course, the whole essay is a piece of fun, but Stevenson had a serious purpose too. A little later on he says:

> Extreme *busyness*, whether at school or college, kirk or market, is a symptom of deficient vitality… As if a man's soul were not too small to begin with, they have dwarfed and narrowed theirs by a life of all work and no play…

Now there, with the mention of the danger of 'extreme busyness' in the kirk, he touches us all to the quick, as witnessed by Mark Vernon's recent *Church Times* opinion piece suggesting that we, who are meant to offer the world those gateways and portals into *Otium Sacrum*, and spiritual largesse, sometimes show symptoms of 'anxiety and manic overwork'.

Idly turning the pages of this defence of idling I find myself hoping that some of the schoolchildren through whose hands it passed took Stevenson's advice. I certainly feel inclined to take it myself!

68

The Oldest Door

I was sitting quietly in the parish church of St Botolph's in Hadstock when the door opened behind me and a friendly local looked in, a warden or verger, I guessed, just checking to see who was in the church today. It is wonderful that these ancient places stand open and unlocked but quite understandable that, in the interest of the fixtures and fittings, neighbours come in to cast a friendly eye on whoever might have wandered in. Sizing me up as an unlikely purloiner of lead roofing or church plate, she took a different tack:

'I expect you've come for The Door', she said.

The door? I hesitated, 'I don't know anything about the door.'

'Ah, well you might like to know that the door you've just walked through is the oldest door in England, and it's often what brings people here'

'Goodness!' I felt a little shiver of delight at the thought of it.

'Well, it's the oldest *working* door', she said, 'the oldest that has been in continuous use. There's a little door in Westminster Abbey, which was once used by Edward the Confessor, but this door was set here, we believe, by King Cnut, in 1022, when the church was built and dedicated to St Botolph with whom this church has even older links. It's been opening and closing for the people of Hadstock and further afield these thousand years, and more, in a way.'

181

'More? What do you mean?'

'Well, this stone church was built over the remains of an older one, a Saxon foundation, perhaps Botolph's own monastery. They did some digging, and found the remains of the wooden church that stood before this one, and they also took some tiny samples from the door, and those revealed that the oak from which this door was hewn may have been alive and growing much earlier still, perhaps as early as 650.'

I was astonished, and, after she left, I walked over and touched the door, just to feel the living root and connection with something green and growing within a generation of St Augustine's arrival at Canterbury. I thought of the long continuity of days and years, through the rise and fall of dynasties, the flourishing and decay of languages, the big historical swings of reformation and revolution, passing like cloud-shadows over this good ground, while day by day this door opened on the changing faces and common faith of a persistent, local, rooted Christian community.

It turns out, perhaps unsurprisingly, that St Botolph is the patron saint of gates and doorways; St Botolph's church in Cambridge stands where the old wall and gate used to be, and, more remarkably, churches at the four old City gates of London; Aldersgate, Bishopsgate, Aldgate and Billingsgate all had dedications to Botolph. And now here in his old East Anglian heartland I felt he was holding open a door for me, though that door was even older than the one Cnut, that penitent Viking, had hung here. For the door through which I had unwittingly passed in St Botolph's was not only a door into a church, but also a door into the One who said, 'I am the door of the sheepfold'; the old oak door I saw still hanging on its hinges in Hadstock was itself only a shadow of the one St John saw in Patmos, when he said, with devastating simplicity:

And I saw a door open in heaven.

69

The Green Man

> My face in the foliage, you've seen that face before
> Carved in the choir by your fathers in days of yore
> I'm the power in the pulse, I'm the song underneath the soil,
> I'm the unseen king of the ditches, ragged and royal …

These lines from my song 'The Green Man' sprang from my fascination with the mysterious carvings of 'foliate heads' in old churches and cathedrals, a motif first named 'The Green Man' in an article in *Folklore* by Julia, Lady Raglan in 1939. It has since become the standard term for the immense variety of these 'faces in the foliage', some mischievous, some numinous, some leering, some wise, and all intriguing. From Southwell Minster, to Kilpeck, from Rosslyn Chapel to Hereford Cathedral, they peer out from their hidden groves of stone and wood. Lady Raglan associated these figures with the folk traditions clustered around 'the figure variously known as The Green Man, Jack-in-the Green, Robin Hood, the King of the May, and the Garland, who is the central figure for May-Day celebrations throughout Northern and Central Europe'. She goes on to suggest that these traditions are themselves the memory of an earlier pre-Christian religion.

There may well be elements of a pagan reverence for the mystery of growth and renewal and for the magic and beauty of the greenwood, woven into the figure of the green man. And rightly so, for *pagan* means at root a dweller in the *pagus,* the field or heath (hence also the word *heathen*). But the fact remains that all of these carvings are to be found in churches and cathedrals; it was the Church that preserved the memory of this earlier reverence, and discerned that these figures also belonged within that delicately carved grove, that forest of light and stone that is gothic architecture. And, again, rightly so, for in Christ 'a greater than Pan is here', and that greatness always includes what it fulfils. The Word in whom all things were made patterned the sign of his death and resurrection into nature itself and pagan reverence for the 'death' of the seed that falls to earth, and its resurrection in golden grain was preparing us in heart and mind to recognize the death and resurrection of the One who said 'unless a grain of wheat falls into the earth and dies it abides alone, but if it dies it brings forth much fruit'. Perhaps those foliate heads from whose mouths spring out the leaves and tendrils of the vine were carved in recognition of the One who said 'I am the Vine; you are the branches.' Orthodox Christians have nothing to fear from an image like the Green Man. Whatever may become of him in the neo-pagan pages of the internet, when he is brought to Christ he flourishes. So I continued, unabashed, weaving a new thread of 'I AM' sayings into my song:

I'm the roots on the stock, I'm the tender shoots on the vine
I'm the goodness in the bread, I'm the wildness in the wine
There's power in the place where my smallest tendrils are curled
And my softest touch is the strongest thing in the world
I'm the Green Man, don't take my name in vain
I'm the Green Man, it's time to break my chain
If you cut me down I'll spring back green again.

70

Emily Dickinson's Desk

I was reflecting the other day on Emily Dickinson's famous lines about effective truth-telling:

> Tell all the Truth but tell it slant –
> Success in Circuit lies
> Too bright for our infirm Delight
> The Truth's superb surprise.

That first line is quoted in many different contexts and I fear that some of those who quote it are more interested in the slant than the truth. Perhaps they forget that the first phrase in that poem is 'Tell *all* the truth'. Like all great poets she will have no truck with those who are 'economic with the actualité'. She is right though about the need to circle, to embody and give gradual form to apprehensions too bright for sight. In the less frequently quoted second verse of that poem she speaks of 'Lightning to the Children eased' and says that truth must 'dazzle gradually/Or every man be blind.'

Perhaps the grace and kindness of the gradual is one of the reasons why we are in the world at all, why we experience things through the medium of time, moment by moment: we cannot cope yet with the fullness of the eternal now. Perhaps too that is why the Light himself became 'Lightning to the Children eased', and was born in a stable.

I was speaking at a conference in Amherst once, and I

had the opportunity to visit Emily Dickinson's house, now beautifully preserved as the Emily Dickinson Museum. It is just as she left it, with the same furniture, the same well-worn stairs, and the same spare and beautiful New England grace. And so I came to stand in that 'mighty room'; the room she scarcely ever left, the room where all the poems were written, and there, plain and simple and strangely, paradoxically small, was her little desk: a square writing table that would hardly hold the width of a modern laptop. I was filled with wonder at how much had flowed from so small a space, but then I thought about Dickinson's characteristically concentrated and terse verse forms; those compact and concentrated little quatrains with the emphatic dashes linking and yet binding-in the energy of her phrases, and it seemed to me the smallness of the desk was itself part of the form of the poetry, part of her gift.

The whole experience stirred me on to this little poem about that writing desk, for which I borrowed her terse and condensed verse form:

So slight and spare a square of wood
Sustains so great a muse–
How plain and flat the door is made
To such a subtle maze.

Perhaps the limits of this desk–
–It's strict restraint of space–
Informed the poet's take and task,
And turned restraint to grace.

Here in this narrow paradise
She pledged and kept her troth–
And trimmed her lamp and trained her verse –
And – slant-wise – told her truth.

71

Smoke Rings

The art of blowing smoke rings, like all true arts, has at its heart a paradox. Poetry finds its freedom in the constraint of form, music suggests the timeless by keeping time, and smoke rings are blown by not being blown at all.

If you try to *blow* a smoke ring you will find that your breath is nothing but eddies and disturbances in the air, disturbances that will pull your ring to pieces before it is even half-formed. The secret is not to breathe out, but to keep the smoke in your mouth as still as the air outside, and then to pop the smoke out gently with your tongue so that your ring floats out whole and pristine, still expanding and gently turning on its own momentum. But it's hard, at first, not to breathe out when you push, so you must be completely relaxed - indeed you must attain a Zen-like calm. And that of course is the whole point of pipe smoking and blowing smoke rings. So I wrote in the opening verse of my poem, 'Smoke Rings From My Pipe':

> All the long day's weariness is done
> I'm free at last to do just as I will,
> Take out my pipe, admire the setting sun,
> Practise the art of simply sitting still.
> Thank God I have this briar bowl to fill,
> I leave the world with all its hopeless hype,
> Its pressures, and its ever-ringing till,
> And let it go in smoke rings from my pipe.

In fact, this poem got me into trouble, when a reviewer of my last poetry book, *Parable and Paradox*, having approved in general of the whole collection, and praised the phrasing of one or two poems, singled this poem out for reproof. How could I spoil a devotional volume with this reprehensible hymn to tobacco, and to the pernicious habit of smoking which we should all now be leaving behind? I felt like the boy who has been caught smoking behind the bike sheds, probably because I once *was* the boy caught smoking behind the bike sheds!

And yes, I know times have changed, and gone are the days when we gathered in the little snug at the back of the pub and smoked our pipes together, when the layers of smoke in the room were so dense that our smoke rings would gather more to themselves as they rolled above the table between us and then suddenly gleam silver in a shaft of sunlight. Gone too are the days when C. S. Lewis could write: 'I believe that many who find that 'nothing happens' when they sit down, or kneel down, to a book of devotion, would find that the heart sings unbidden while they are working their way through a tough bit of theology with a pipe in their teeth and a pencil in their hand.'

Though I cherish those old memories I am genuinely glad that the smoke has cleared from the pubs, and I am content that my pipe should become more and more a solitary pleasure, confined to the shrine of my writing hut, the Temple of Peace. Nevertheless I am still bold to pray the prayer with which I ended that poem:

Prince, I have done with grinding at the mill,

These petty-pelting tyrants aren't my type,
So lift me up and set me on a hill,
A free man blowing smoke rings from his pipe.

72

A Lens

We have all occasionally to endure the odd jibe or scoff from those whom Schleiermacher so generously calls 'the cultured despisers of religion', though some of them are not so cultured as they imagine. Most of these jibes and scoffs are so shallow and inane as to be scarcely worthy of a response, but respond we must and with as much courtesy and grace as we can muster. My current least favourite is: 'Oh you religious people, you think you've got God in a box!' When this is uttered in a place like Ely Cathedral, as it was in my hearing not long ago, one is tempted to gesture upwards into the numinous blent air of this spacious palace of light, to glance at the delicate tracery of its arches and windows, and say, 'Well, at least it's a better box than the windowless warehouses where your little gods are stored.' But of course one says no such thing. One makes a silent prayer for patience and charity, and tries instead to explain that we have never claimed to keep God in a box, that even at the dedication of the Temple Solomon had exclaimed 'Behold, the heaven and heaven of heavens cannot contain thee; how much less this house that I have builded?' and that likewise the shapes and containers we have made with words, or even with thoughts, cannot contain the fullness of his mystery, and no one has ever claimed that they could. Even C.S. Lewis, who is just the kind of Christian these cultured persons like to despise, had said:

Thoughts are but coins. Let me not trust instead

Of Thee, their thin-worn image of Thy head.
From all my thoughts, even from my thoughts of Thee,
O thou fair Silence, fall, and set me free.

And one tries too, a positive tack, a fuller account of what a sacred building really is. One points out that life and beauty, as gifts from God, are everywhere around us but that sometimes it takes a particular lens to bring them into focus. Sacred architecture, one patiently explains, is a little like a lens, made by people wiser than we are, to help us at least to glimpse a little of what we might otherwise miss, of the God who is everywhere. Prayers, scriptures and religious rites are something like that too.

I have been called to account by the scoffers so often that I ended up trying to crystallize and condense my response to this particular jibe into the 14 lines of a sonnet; it seemed marginally better than simply biting my tongue.

A Lens

Not that we think he is confined to us,
Locked in the box of our religious rites,
Or curtained by these frail cathedral walls,
No church is broad or creed compendious
Enough. All thought's a narrowing of sites,
Before him every definition fails,
Words fall and flutter into emptiness,
Like motes of dust within his spaciousness.
Not that we summon him, but that he lends
The very means whereby he might be known,

Till this opacity of stone on stone,
This trace of light and music on the air,
This sacred space itself becomes a lens
To sense his presence who is everywhere.

73

St. Fillan's Cave

The other day I made a pilgrimage to the little fishing village of Pittenweem in the East Neuk of Fife. While Anstruther, a short but vigorous walk along the coast, has the Scottish Fisheries Museum, with its wonderful old vessels, lovingly restored, a testimony to the skill, courage and culture of Scots fisher-folk, it is Pittenweem that still has the working boats, and here, what you glimpsed in the museum up the coast is a lived reality. Much as I took delight in the boats moored up by the harbour fish-market, it was something older still that had drawn me to this little village: it was St Fillan's Cave.

It's a remarkable place. Over countless years a river in the limestone rocks and the strong action of the sea itself combined to hollow out a long passage into the rock whose walls and roofs are all water-sculpted into graceful whorls and curves. Then a change in sea level left the cave high enough above the shoreline to be habitable, or at least serviceable, first to St Fillan, a seventh-century Celtic missionary to the Picts, and later to other hermits, from the Abbey on the Island of May, coming here for contemplation but also serving pilgrims on route to or from the Holy Shrine of St Andrews. For some centuries the cave was covered over and forgotten until a ploughman, breaking the ground above it, found a hidden stone stair leading down to this secret haven, and it was rediscovered, cleaned and re-opened and is now once more a place of prayer.

You enter through a little gate, set with a sign of the cross and descend gently towards a ledge set with a painting of Fillan himself, with a companion saint. He bears a quill in his right hand and round his neck a little satchel for an ink bottle. His left arm, raised in blessing, haloed and bright, recalls the legend that when he needed to write in the darkness of his cave his left arm became radiant with divine light while he wrote with his right. A little way in past this image, the cave divides into two further chambers, breathing and echoing like lungs, or like the chambers of the heart. At the entrance to the right-hand chamber is set a stone altar with a cross, but the other is left free, just as the sea sculpted it, with a round still pool on the stone floor into which, every so often, a single drop falls from the roof above, making beautiful ripple patterns and a small musical note taken up by the echoes of the cave, until the pool is still and the cave silent again.

You can sit there in the quiet, contemplating the right hand of your activity, your religious making and shaping, but also drawing deeply from the left, the natural pool, open receptive, accepting in stillness from above a quiet, rhythmic, raindrop of blessing.

When the plough broke through above this hidden cave, the village remembered the forgotten meaning of its own name; for Pittenweem means 'the place of the cave'. So it is with us, we plough on with our business, day after day, forgetting who we are, until some small breakdown becomes a breakthrough, and we return at last to a place of prayer in the forgotten chambers of the heart.